SpringerBriefs in Public Health

SpringerBriefs in Public Health present concise summaries of cutting-edge research and practical applications from across the entire field of public health, with contributions from medicine, bioethics, health economics, public policy, biostatistics, and sociology.

The focus of the series is to highlight current topics in public health of interest to a global audience, including health care policy; social determinants of health; health issues in developing countries; new research methods; chronic and infectious disease epidemics; and innovative health interventions.

Featuring compact volumes of 50 to 125 pages, the series covers a range of content from professional to academic. Possible volumes in the series may consist of timely reports of state-of-the art analytical techniques, reports from the field, snapshots of hot and/or emerging topics, elaborated theses, literature reviews, and in-depth case studies. Both solicited and unsolicited manuscripts are considered for publication in this series.

Briefs are published as part of Springer's eBook collection, with millions of users worldwide. In addition, Briefs are available for individual print and electronic purchase.

Briefs are characterized by fast, global electronic dissemination, standard publishing contracts, easy-to-use manuscript preparation and formatting guidelines, and expedited production schedules. We aim for publication 8–12 weeks after acceptance.

More information about this series at http://www.springer.com/series/10138

Rocco Palumbo

The Bright Side and the Dark Side of Patient Empowerment

Co-creation and Co-destruction of Value in the Healthcare Environment

Springer

Rocco Palumbo
Department of Management and Innovation
   Systems
University of Salerno
Fisciano
Italy

ISSN 2192-3698   ISSN 2192-3701   (electronic)
SpringerBriefs in Public Health
ISBN 978-3-319-58343-3   ISBN 978-3-319-58344-0   (eBook)
DOI 10.1007/978-3-319-58344-0

Library of Congress Control Number: 2017939308

Printed on acid-free paper

This Springer imprint is published by Springer Nature
The registered company is Springer International Publishing AG
The registered company address is: Gewerbestrasse 11, 6330 Cham, Switzerland

To Anna,
To whom I owe all that I know

Foreword

Patient empowerment is a delicate issue for scholars and practitioners interested in public health. Many studies have discussed the different shades which build this construct, providing a wide array of conceptual perspectives from which patient empowerment could be investigated. Far from paving the way for a consistent and agreed definition of patient empowerment, the growing scientific interest in this field has produced a large number of competing definitions, to the point that patient empowerment may mean various things for different audiences.

From this point of view, writing a brief which aims at providing a synoptic view of patient empowerment may be a challenging task. Rocco Palumbo undertook this effort and I was fascinated when I read the first proof of this book.

An in-depth examination of patient empowerment is pointed out, which concerns both the bright and the dark sides of the process of patient involvement in the delivery of health services. On the one hand, patient empowerment may lead to the awakening of sleeping resources, thus contributing to a more appropriate access to care and better health outcomes. On the other hand, there is a significant risk that the engagement of patients in the design and delivery of care may turn into value co-destruction. This is especially common when either patients lack the basic functional, interactive and critical health-related skills to properly navigate the healthcare service system or healthcare organizations are not able to establish friendly and co-creating relationships with the patients. Drawing on these considerations, the enhancement of individual and organizational health literacy should be recognized as a fundamental strategy to realize the full potential of patient empowerment initiatives.

Health policy makers and managers of healthcare organizations may benefit from reading this brief. In fact, it provides an overview of the role played by patient empowerment in inspiring the future shapes of the healthcare service system, thus informing both strategic and organizational decisions aimed at involving the patients in value co-creation. Besides, healthcare professionals may appreciate this book, which suggests a recipe for the effective implementation of patient empowerment initiatives. Last but not least, this book inspires an agenda for future research, encouraging scholars to investigate the attributes of patient empowerment interventions and the consequences which could derive.

Ultimately, this book is an effective synthesis of the current state of the art of the scientific knowledge in the field of patient empowerment, paving the way for further developments aimed at pushing forward the understanding of the specific attributes and effects of initiatives intended to empower patients.

Salerno, Italy   Paola Adinolfi
February, 2017

Preface

Patient empowerment is a hot topic in healthcare management and public health, which is attracting the growing interest of scholars and practitioners. However, there is still little agreement on what is meant by patient empowerment. Moreover, little is known about the distinguishing attributes and the consequences of patient empowerment interventions. Drawing on these considerations, this brief aims at pushing forward the knowledge in the field of patient empowerment, in an attempt to fill the current gaps in the scientific literature. For these purposes, it discusses the positive role of patient empowerment in shaping the healthcare service system of the future; besides, it investigates the "dark side" of patient empowerment, examining the risks of value co-destruction which could be attached to the engagement of patients in the delivery of care.

As compared with the existing literature, this brief strives for providing the reader with a full-fledged understanding of the patient empowerment concept. On the one hand, patient empowerment is depicted as a paradigm shift from the traditional bio-medical/industrial model of care toward a patient-centered approach, which is largely consistent with the contents of the healthcare reforms of most of Western countries. On the other hand, the side effects of patient empowerment are dealt with, emphasizing that patient involvement in the design and delivery of care may result in the misuse of available resources. This is especially true when the patients and the healthcare professionals bring contrasting expectations, conflicting inputs and diverging ends in the healthcare environment, paving the way for value co-destruction.

Rather than focusing on the implementation issues of patient empowerment in a specific healthcare setting—such as primary care or hospital care—this book conceives patient empowerment as a mainstream strategy, which is able to deeply affect the future shapes of the healthcare service system. Notwithstanding, this brief is not biased by an excessively optimistic interpretation of patient empowerment. As anticipated, it delves into both the bright and the dark sides of patient empowerment, in order to identify the key ingredients which should be included in the recipe for effective patient empowerment. From this point of view, this book is not targeted to a specific audience. Rather, it is addressed to the general public of students, scholars and practitioners who are interested in healthcare management and public health. Among others, health policy makers, senior managers of healthcare organizations and healthcare professionals may benefit from reading this brief.

The book is organized in four chapters, which are strictly intertwined. Chapter 1 introduces the main topic of the volume. In particular, it provides the reader with a contextualization of patient empowerment, pointing out the key attributes which build this construct. The roots of the patient empowerment concept are outlined. Moreover, the different perspectives suggested by the scientific literature to deal with this construct are investigated, in an attempt to devise an overarching definition of patient empowerment. In light of this conceptual framework, the requisites to patient empowerment interventions are discussed, embracing a relational interpretation. In fact, the effective implementation of patient empowerment initiatives does not solely rely on the enablement of patients; rather, it requires the enhancement of the healthcare organizations' ability to establish a friendly and co-creating relationship with the patients.

Chapter 2 delves into the bright side of patient empowerment. First of all, it builds a conceptual link between patient empowerment and value co-creation. Empowered patients are considered to be more willing to participate in health decision making and to establish a co-creating partnership with the providers of care. In other words, patient empowerment reframes the patient-provider relationship, identifying the former as an active agent rather than as a sheer consumer of health services. Therefore, patient empowerment is argued to be an antecedent of health services' co-production. Actually, empowered patients are more willing to be involved in the design and delivery of care, thus performing as service co-producers. Patient involvement allows a better distribution of responsibilities between the patients and the providers of care, reducing the inappropriate access to care and enhancing health outcomes. Hence, patient empowerment initiatives may pave the way for lower healthcare costs and increased sustainability of the healthcare service system.

Chapter 3 discusses the dark side of patient empowerment. Drawing from the most recent conceptual developments in the fields of service science and healthcare management, patient empowerment is claimed to be not enough to realize patient engagement. In fact, patient empowerment does not necessarily produce the involvement of the patient in the provision of care, if it is not associated with a process of patient enablement. Empowered patients who are not able or unwilling to actively participate in the design and delivery of care are at risk of co-destroying value. Sticking to these considerations, a need for enlightening the dark side of patient empowerment is argued, in an attempt to devise and implement appropriate strategies intended to overcome the barriers to value co-creation in the healthcare service system.

The concluding Chap. 4 points out the role of health literacy in empowering patients. Health literacy is presented as a multifaceted concept, which shows an individual and an organizational shade. On the one hand, individual health literacy concerns the patients' ability to access, understand, process and use health information, in order to navigate the healthcare environment properly. On the other hand, organizational health literacy involves the capacity of the healthcare organizations to establish a clear and comfortable setting, which fosters the willingness of the patients and the healthcare professionals to build a co-creating partnership. Both individual and organizational health literacy are considered to be fundamental ingredients of the recipe for effective patient empowerment interventions.

This brief has been written by a single author. However, many people contributed—either directly or indirectly—in its accomplishment. I am aware that any acknowledgement would be insufficient to thank those who supported me in conceiving and writing this work. However, a special gratitude goes to Anna, my mother, to whom this book is dedicated. She encouraged me during each step of my academic career and I owe to her my passion for research. Also, I have to thank Matteo, my father, and Carmela, my sister, who have always doubted my skills and have incited me to do my best to succeed. I owe to Prof. Paola Adinolfi, my landmark in the academic world, and to Prof. Elio Borgonovi, my scientific benchmark, the interest for patient empowerment and value co-creation in the healthcare environment: without them, this book would have not been written. My sincere gratitude goes to Carmela Annarumma, Marilena Indrieri and Gabriella Piscopo for their kind friendship and their help in completing this brief. Especially, I am obliged to Martina Saviano, who comfortably cares for me when troubles arise and when things go wrong, as only a trusted friend is able to do. Also, thank you, Teresa: you taught me what is hate and pain, disempowering me in the most difficult period of my life. In your deep silence I retrieved the worst expression of mankind. Last but not least, I owe to you the strength to go on: thank you, Rosalba.

Fisciano, Italy   Rocco Palumbo

Contents

About the Author

Rocco Palumbo is a Licensed Associate Professor and Research Fellow in Organizational Studies at the Department of Management and Innovation Systems of the University of Salerno, where he achieved his Ph.D. in Economics and Management of Public Sector Organizations. His main research areas include, but are not limited to, organizational health literacy, individual health literacy, patient empowerment, service co-production, value co-creation, and human resource management. He published many articles examining the special attributes of health literate healthcare organizations and investigating the consequences of limited health literacy on both health services' utilization and health outcomes. Prior to joining the University of Salerno, Rocco Palumbo served as a volunteer for several international charity organizations operating in the fields of health promotion and prevention. During this activity, he led different projects in Tanzania (East Africa) and the Federal Democratic Republic of Nepal (South Asia) concerning the access of disadvantaged young to adequate education.

List of Figures

List of Tables

Chapter 1
Contextualizing Patient Empowerment

1.1 Toward a Tentative Definition of Patient Empowerment

The traditional understanding of healthcare relies on a biomedical/industrial model, which conceives the patient as a sheer consumer of health services and emphasizes the role of healthcare professionals as the sole value creators in the healthcare environment. The myths of objectivity (Wilson, 2000) and rationality (Ashcroft & Van Katwyk, 2016) have been argued to be the main underpinnings of biomedicine, involving a strict focus on the clinical treatment of the disease. However, these myths produced the establishment of a biased relationship between the patients and the healthcare professionals, which is based on professional dominance (Freidson, 1970).

Even though the biomedical model of care has been considered to be the "*dominant paradigm of twentieth century medicine*" (Callahan & Pincus, 1997, p. 283), the challenges raised by both practitioners and scholars against it are deeply rooted (Longino & Murphy, 1995). Among others, Engel (1989, p. 39) blamed the biomedical paradigm of leaving no space "*for the social, psychological, and behavioral dimensions of illness*". As a consequence, it is able to prevent a full-fledged understanding of both health determinants and patients' health needs, thus undermining the appropriateness of care.

The shift toward patient-centered care could be understood as an attempt to question the timeliness and the effectiveness of the biomedical approach to care (Epstein & Street, 2011). In fact, patient-centered care strives for recognizing the person behind the patient (Ekman et al., 2011), in order to fully address his or her specific health and/or social needs and to improve the quality of care (Bechtel & Ness, 2010). Drawing on these considerations, a growing attention has been paid to patient-centered care. Several scholars have pointed out that it variously contributes in: reducing health-related costs (Bertakis & Azari, 2011), enhancing health outcomes (Rathert, Wyrwich, & Boren, 2013), and increasing patients' satisfaction

© The Author(s) 2017
P. Rocco, *The Bright Side and the Dark Side of Patient Empowerment*,
SpringerBriefs in Public Health, DOI 10.1007/978-3-319-58344-0_1

(de Boer, Delnoij, & Rademakers, 2013). Nonetheless, patient-centered care could not be realized if the patients are not encouraged to develop adequate health competencies in order to actively participate in co-designing and co-delivering health services (Bernabeo & Holmboe, 2013).

In line with these points, the scientific literature has discussed the complex relationship which links patient-centered care and patient empowerment, depicting them as complementary concepts (Holmström & Röing, 2010). On the one hand, patient-centered care implies a process of patient empowerment, in an attempt to inspire the design and the delivery of care to the patients' specific health needs. On the other hand, patient empowerment involves a reconfiguration of the relationships between the healthcare professionals and the patients, stimulating the shift toward a patient-centered approach to care (Anderson & Funnell, 2005). Sticking to these considerations, it could be maintained that patient empowerment is an important ingredient of the recipe for the transition from the traditional biomedical model to a patient-centered approach to care (Gachoud, Albert, Kuper, Stroud, & Reeves, 2012).

It is not easy to provide a comprehensive definition of patient empowerment. According to the prevailing scientific literature, empowerment is a process which is aimed at increasing the individual ability to deal with everyday issues, allowing people to gain mastery over their own life affairs (Rappaport, 1987). When it is attached to the peculiar experience of patients in the healthcare service system, the process of empowerment concerns the individual ability to gain control over health-related decisions. Hence, patient empowerment involves the achievement of a balance of power between the healthcare professionals and the patients (Elwyn, Edwards, & Thompson, 2016). Patient empowerment could be depicted as a cognitive process, which is based on patients' awareness, self-confidence, engagement and control (Kaldoudi & Makris, 2015). To be empowered, the patients should be adequately informed of their health-related conditions, willing to participate in the delivery of care and actively involved in health decision making.

Echoing these arguments, patient empowerment has been described as an enabling process (Chatzimarkakis, 2010). In fact, it allows to awaken the sleeping resources of patients, in order to encourage their participation in the provision of care and to pave the way for value co-creation (Palumbo, 2016a). In other words, patient empowerment leads toward the establishment of a co-creating partnership between the healthcare providers and the patients (Bravo et al., 2015). The former strive for enabling the patients and inciting their active participation in the provision of care. At the same time, the latter are motivated to perform as self-determining agents, who are responsible for their health-related decisions and obtain a sufficient level of control over their interaction with the healthcare professionals (Funnell & Anderson, 2004).

Even though patient empowerment turns out to be consistent with the paradigm shift from biomedicine to patient-centered care, it is worth noting that its implementation is affected by a series of misconceptions which are attached to it (Anderson & Funnell, 2010). In fact, the clash between the theory and the practice of patient empowerment has been duly investigated in the scientific literature, resulting in a cacophony, rather than a polysemy (Aujoulat, d'Hoore, & Deccache, 2007). This clash is often produced by the attempt of healthcare professionals to maintain their control over the healthcare delivery system, which is not consistent with the conceptualization of patient empowerment as an enabling process (Williams, 2002). As reported by Anderson and Funnell (2010, p. 277), patient empowerment requires that the healthcare providers make an effort to "*increase the capacity of patients to think critically*" about health-related issues and to make autonomous and informed decisions in navigating the healthcare environment.

In an attempt to systematize these different perspectives, patient empowerment could be understood as a relational—rather than an individual—construct. Indeed, it is established in the relationship between the patients and the healthcare providers and relies on the commitment of both the parties to implement a patient-centered approach to care. For this purpose, the healthcare professionals should dismiss their loyalty to the traditional biomedical model, which conceives them as healers who embrace a fix-it approach to care (Adinolfi, 2014). Quite the opposite, they should perform as carers, who facilitate the patients' autonomy and self-determination (Barry & Edgman-Levitan, 2012). Concomitantly, the patients should be aware of their potential role in co-creating value within the healthcare service system; as well, they should be willing to actively participate in the provision of care, co-planning, co-designing, and co-delivering health services.

A process of patient enablement is needed to enact such a co-creating partnership between the patients and the healthcare professionals, which allows to match the individual knowledge and skills with the requirements for patient involvement. As a result of such an enabling process, the patients are able to take an active role in making appropriate health decisions and implementing them (Asimakopoulou, Gilbert, Newton, & Scambler, 2012). Figure 1.1 provides a graphical synthesis of the proposed relational interpretation of patient empowerment: it is worth noting that patient empowerment is assumed to be a circular and iterative process, which benefits from the establishment of a long-term partnership between the patients and the healthcare providers.

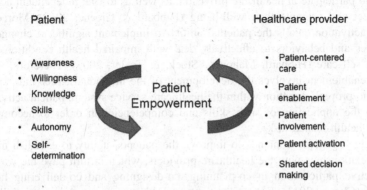

Patient

Healthcare provider

- Awareness
- Willingness
- Knowledge
- Skills
- Autonomy
- Self-determination

Patient Empowerment

- Patient-centered care
- Patient enablement
- Patient involvement
- Patient activation
- Shared decision making

Fig. 1.1 The relational interpretation of patient empowerment. *Source* Author's elaboration

1.2   The Different Flavors of Patient Empowerment

Patient empowerment is a multifaceted concept, which may have different meanings to various audiences (Roberts, 1999). From this standpoint, is not surprising that patient empowerment has been usually confused with similar, but distinct concepts, which aim at implementing a patient-centered approach to care. As anticipated in the previous section, patient empowerment could be conceived as both a process and an outcome (Anderson & Funnell, 2010). On the one hand, it involves an enabling process, which is intended to improve the patients' ability to participate in value co-creation (Aujoulat, Marcolongo, Bonadiman, & Deccache, 2008). On the other hand, it allows the patients to obtain control over their health-related conditions and to be aware of the available resources in the healthcare service system to protect and promote their psycho-physical well-being (Funnell et al., 1991).

In light of these points, it is not surprising that patient empowerment has been argued to overlap with various constructs which share the same purposes of patient empowerment, such as: patient enablement, patient activation, patient engagement, and patient involvement. Fumagalli, Radaelli, Lettieri, Bertele', and Masella (2015) tried to mark the boundaries between patient empowerment and its correlates, in an attempt to achieve a better understanding of what is needed to empower the patients.

Patient enablement and patient activation could be claimed to be the preconditions to patient empowerment. In particular, patient enablement concerns the patients' feelings of confidence in navigating the healthcare environment and interacting with the healthcare providers. It affects the individual ability to cope with health and illness, in order to increase the individual well-being (Mead, Bower, & Roland, 2008). In other words, patient enablement focuses on the improvement of the individual knowledge, skills and attitudes which are required to balance the power between the patients and the providers of care (Pawlikowska, Zhang, Griffiths, van Dalen, & van der Vleuten, 2012).

Patient activation is peculiar in that it puts into action the health-related knowledge and skills of patients. In fact, it concerns their willingness and factual ability to participate in healthcare provision, as well as to take independent actions to protect and promote their well-being (Hibbard & Greene, 2013). Moreover, patient activation entails the patients' ability to implement significant changes in life-styles and behaviors to effectively deal with impaired health conditions and achieve self-care (Hibbard, Mahoney, Stock, & Tusler, 2007). Therefore, while patient enablement involves the development of the individual skills and competencies to properly function within the healthcare service system, patient activation aims to the application of such skills and competencies in order to accomplish specific health-related tasks.

Patient engagement intends to improve the patients' ability to establish meaningful relationships with the healthcare providers, which in turn pave the way for their active participation in co-planning, co-designing and co-delivering health services (Clancy, 2011). Engaged patients are able to set up a therapeutic alliance with the providers of care (Simpson, 2004), which contributes in enhancing their self-effectiveness and their willingness to participate in processes of value co-creation (Palumbo, 2016a). Patient engagement is a key responsibility of healthcare professionals, who should make the patients aware of their critical role in the provision of care and encourage their active participation in health-related decision making (Gruman et al., 2010).

Patient involvement could be understood as an advanced stage of patient engagement. Involved patients recognize their power in the user-provider relationship and participate at the different stages of the healthcare delivery process (Thompson, 2007). From this point of view, patient involvement leads toward the establishment of a full-fledged co-creating partnership between the patients and the healthcare providers, which results in shared health decision making (Barry & Edgman-Levitan, 2012) and health services' co-production (Palumbo, 2016a). In sum, patient involvement implies a complete shift toward patient-centered care, even though within the institutional limits that regulate the functioning of the healthcare service system (Jones et al., 2004).

Patient enablement, patient activation, patient engagement and patient involvement could be considered to be mutually related. In addition, they could be depicted as a specific shade of the broader patient empowerment construct. In other words, patient empowerment is a complex and participatory process, which aims at improving the health-related knowledge, skills, attitudes and expertise of patients, in order to raise their awareness of their co-creating potential in the delivery of care. Ultimately, patient empowerment is aimed at enhancing the patients' willingness and ability to establish an alliance with the healthcare professionals and to make informed decisions in the healthcare environment (Hain & Dianne, 2013; Salmon & Hall, 2003; Small, Bower, Chew-Graham, Whalley, & Protheroe, 2013).

Figure 1.2 summarizes these points, providing a graphical representation of the relationships between patient empowerment and its related concepts. An enabling process is at the basis of patient empowerment initiatives. Patients need to improve their health-related knowledge and competencies, in order to participate in the

Fig. 1.2 The relationship between patient empowerment and its related concepts. *Source* Author's elaboration

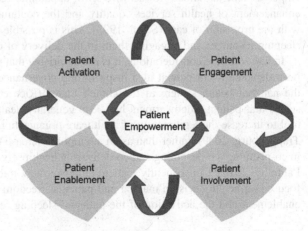

provision of care. However, knowledge is not enough. The patients should be encouraged to play an active role in the healthcare service system. For this purpose, an enablement process is required, which is intended to raise the patients' awareness of their potential contribution in value co-creation and to increase their willingness to co-produce health services.

Patient enablement and patient activation awaken the sleeping assets of patients and set the conditions for their engagement in co-planning, co-designing and co-delivering health services. In turn, patient engagement relies on the establishment of a co-creating partnership between the healthcare providers and the patients, which paves the way for a full-fledged involvement of the latter in health decision making. As anticipated, each of these steps generates a particular shade of patient empowerment, improving the patients' ability to perform as value co-creators in the healthcare environment. In addition, patient empowerment activates a self-nourishing virtuous cycle, which could be argued to increase the participation of patients in co-planning, co-designing and co-delivering health services.

1.3 Patient Empowerment in Health Reform: A Snapshot of the State of the Art in Western Countries

Sticking to the biomedical model, a paternalistic approach to care seems to prevail in the healthcare environment (Colombo, Moja, Gonzalez-Lorenzo, Liberati, & Mosconi, 2012). Nevertheless, patient empowerment has been claimed to play an important role in molding the future shapes of healthcare systems across the World (Whitehead, Hanratty, & Popay, 2010; Sminkey, 2013). While several scholars have attached a mere consumerist label to patient empowerment (Huckman & Kelley, 2013), the involvement of patients in healthcare provision has been widely understood as a strategic approach intended to enhance the overall functioning of the healthcare service system (Pelletier & Stichler, 2013). In particular, patient empowerment is aimed to achieve two apparently competing purposes: the enhancement of health services' quality and the containment of costs associated with the provision of care (Segal, 1998). This is possible by enabling the patients' sleeping resources and engaging them in the delivery of care as value co-creators.

In light of these considerations, it is not surprising that patient empowerment has been depicted as an crucial idea inspiring the governance and the organization of the national health system in the United States (Rice et al., 2013). However, it seems that patient empowerment has been generally dealt with as an instrumental tool to increase the legitimation of healthcare organizations (van de Bovenkamp & Trappenburg, 2009), rather than as an attempt to increase the patients' participation in co-planning, co-designing and co-delivering health services (Adinolfi, Starace, & Palumbo, 2016). Consequently, patient empowerment initiatives have been mainly focused on health decision making and patients' freedom of choice, neglecting the enablement and the activation of the patients' sleeping resources.

In a quite similar way, patient empowerment is assuming a growing relevance in Canada, even though such an interest has not been translated in a greater involvement of the patients in the provision of care (Marchildon, 2013). Most of the attention has been paid on the process of patient enablement and activation, with a strong emphasis on the need for providing the patients with timely and easy to understand health information materials, in an attempt to support their appropriate access to care (Bella, 2010). On the other hand, the limited willingness of the patients to participate in the provision of care and the prevalence of inadequate health literacy have been argued to negatively affect the transition toward patient-centered care in the Canadian context (Canadian Council on Learning, 2007).

Also, patient empowerment is a constitutive elements of health reform in Australia, where it is attached to the purpose of increasing the patients' role in enhancing the functioning of the healthcare service system (Bauman, Fardy, & Harris, 2003). However, as in the American case, a consumerist perspective has been embraced in making the point for patient empowerment, emphasizing the patients' freedom of choice rather than the involvement of the latter in the design and delivery of care. The more frequent use of the construct "consumer empowerment" as compared with "patient empowerment" in institutional documents upholds this consideration (Healy, Sharman, & Lokuge, 2006). In other words, while the access of patients to easy-to-understand health information materials and to comprehensive care have been stressed, little efforts have been addressed to the processes of patients' enablement and activation (Bennett, 2013).

In general, European Countries have devoted significant efforts to underline the importance of patient-centeredness and patient empowerment in restructuring their healthcare systems. In the United Kingdom, patient empowerment has been widely understood as a key strategy to promote the patients' rights to adequate and equal care (Cylus et al., 2015). Among others, the "Expert Patient" policy is intended to awaken the sleeping resources of patients, in order to engage them in healthcare delivery system by virtue of the establishment of a co-creating partnership with the providers of care (Wilson, 2001). In this specific case, patient empowerment does not solely rely on patient choice; rather, it covers the different stages of health services co-production, paving the way for a full-fledged patient involvement in the appropriate functioning of the healthcare service system (Jilka, Callahan, Sevdalis, Mayer, & Darzi, 2015).

Scandinavian Countries share several common traits with the United Kingdom. Patient empowerment represents one of the cornerstones of the Norwegian national health system, which provides the patients with both freedom of choice and involvement in healthcare delivery (Ringard, Sagan, Sperre Saunes, & Lindahl, 2013). The same is true in Sweden, where specific initiatives have been launched in order to: improve equity in the access to care, increase patient choice, enhance the access of patients to health-related information, strengthen the patients' position in the healthcare arena, and encourage a better exchange of information between the healthcare providers and the patients (Anell, Glenngård, & Merkur, 2012). Similarly, patient empowerment has been depicted as a critical policy issue to realize increased effectiveness and cost savings in the Finnish healthcare system, to the point that patient empowerment has been considered to greatly contribute in its long-term sustainability (Vuorenkoski, Mladovsky, & Mossialos, 2008). In these cases, patient empowerment is understood as an attempt to realize the shift from the traditional provider-led model to a patient-centered approach to care, where patients gain control over the most important decisions which concern their health conditions.

The promotion of patients' self-determination characterizes the experience of Denmark (Olejaz et al., 2012) and Germany (Busse & Blümel, 2014). In both the cases, recent health reform have shown a focus on the need to establish the institutional, organizational and operational conditions to realize patient empowerment and to allow the patients to co-create value in collaboration with the healthcare professionals. In France, the merge between patient empowerment and self-determination has been claimed to pave the way for a sort of "health democracy", according to which the patients are considered to perform as the key players in the healthcare service system (Chevreul, Berg Brigham, Durand-Zaleski, & Hernández-Quevedo, 2015). As well, patient participation is dealt with as a fundamental policy priority in Netherland, where health policies are consistent in emphasizing the patients' right to be engaged in health decisions making and to complain about the quality of health services (Kroneman et al., 2016). An analogous situation can be retrieved in Belgium, where recent health reform have emphasized the importance of patient involvement at both the individual and the collective levels. In particular, the right of individual patients and patients' association to participate in framing the future shapes of the healthcare service system has been stressed, sticking to a comprehensive process of patient empowerment, which goes beyond the delivery of care (Gerkens & Merkur, 2010).

As compared with other European States, Mediterranean Countries seem to lag behind in terms of policies and initiatives aimed at empowering the patients. On the one hand, several countries—such as Spain (García-Armesto, Abadía-Taira, Durán, Hernández-Quevedo, & Bernal-Delgado, 2010) and Portugal (Barros, Machado, & Simões, 2011)—have not put a particular emphasis on the institutional and organizational initiatives intended to increase the patients' role and the responsibilities in the healthcare service system. However, they strived for promoting the enhancement of the patients' health-related knowledge and skills, in order to encourage their involvement in the provision of care. On the other hand, some Countries—including Italy (Ferré et al., 2014) and Greece (Economou, 2010)—have not been able to implement effective patient empowerment initiatives, due to the lack of focus in health reform and the inadequate coordination between health and social policies. As a consequence, the need for patient empowerment has been recognized at the institutional level, but it did not turn in practical interventions aimed at involving the patients in value co-creation.

Eastern European Countries are still far from recognizing the potential of patient empowerment in health reform. In most of the cases, only the patients' right to information has been contemplated. This is the case of Romania (Vlădescu, Scîntee, Olsavszky, Hernández-Quevedo, & Sagan, 2016), where the patients are entitled to access comparative information about the quality of healthcare providers, as well as data on medical errors; alternatively, they do not have the access to adequate information on hospital clinical outcomes or waiting times. The same is true in Croatia, where, recent institutional arrangements have been aimed at establishing the right of patients to accept or refuse specific health services and to access reliable health information (Džakula, Sagan, Pavić, Lončarek, & Sekelj-Kauzlarić, 2014). In spite of these considerations, the role of patients in co-creating value has been recognized and promoted in several Countries, including Latvia (Mitenbergs et al., 2012) and Czech Republic (Alexa et al., 2015), where the patients are encouraged to actively participate in the design and delivery of care, in order to improve the quality and effectiveness of health services.

Looking at this snapshot, patient empowerment could be argued to be a recurring topic of health reform in most of the Western Countries. However, it assumes different meanings and specific characteristics in light of the particular attributes of the healthcare system to which it is attached. Therefore, it is not surprising that different instruments have been suggested to achieve patient empowerment. The following section delves into these various approaches, in an attempt to suggest a recipe to realize patient empowerment.

1.4   A Recipe for Patient Empowerment?

The lack of a unanimous definition of patient empowerment has produced a lot of confusion among scholars and practitioners, to the point that it is still not clear who is able to empower whom in the healthcare service system (The Lancet, 2012). It is not surprising that different recipes have been suggested to realize the full potential of patient empowerment. In most of the cases, tailored models to empower people who live with specific health conditions—such as diabetes and hypertension—have been proposed (Distiller, Brown, Joffe, & Kramer, 2010; Wan, Vo, & Barnes, 2012). Alternatively, cross-disease models intended to widely involve the patients in the delivery of care are still poorly discussed from both a conceptual and an empirical point of view (Prigge, Dietz, Homburg, Hoyer, & Burton, 2015).

In general terms, the improvement of the patients' cognitive ability and self-confidence to participate in health decision making has been identified as an important factor to enhance the individual willingness to be engaged in the provision of care (Small et al., 2013). In line with these points, several authors have claimed that patient empowerment begins with knowledge (McGuckin & Govednik, 2014). In fact, the capability of the patients to access, obtain and process health information, their commitment to the improvement of the individual psycho-physical well-being, the adoption of a collaborative approach in the delivery of care and the tolerance of uncertainty have been depicted as key requisites to empower patients and to involve them in a co-creating relationship with the healthcare professionals (Johnson, Rose, Dilworth, & Neilands, 2012; Topac &

Stoicu-Tivadar, 2013). However, the enablement of patients' knowledge and cog-nitive skills is not enough to realize their active involvement in the healthcare delivery system. Once enabled, the cognitive skills of patients need to be activated. For this purpose, a positive patient-provider relationship is crucial (Rowland & Politi, 2016). In fact, the establishment of a friendly and comfortable climate during the medical encounter increases the patients' awareness of their role in co-planning, co-designing and co-delivering health services, paving the way for greater self-efficacy perception and, consequently, stronger engagement (Chiauzzi et al., 2016).

From this point of view, the implementation of a patient-centered approach to care has been generally identified as an important antecedent of patient empow-erment. Patient-centered care entails a radical emancipatory process (Piper, 2010), which relies on the establishment of a therapeutic alliance between the patients and the healthcare professionals (Chatzimarkakis, 2010). Besides, it encourages the patients' active participation in the protection and the promotion of the individual psycho-physical well-being. Such an active participation is possible by stimulating the patients' self-determination and self-efficacy, in order to allow them to be in control over health-related issues and to be able to make autonomous, timely and appropriate health decisions (Dowling, Murphy, Cooney, & Casey, 2011).

Sticking to these considerations, it could be argued that patient empowerment is based on five building blocks (McAllister, Dunn, Payne, Davies, & Todd, 2012): (1) cognitive control, that is to say the awareness of individual health-related conditions and the knowledge about the resources available in the healthcare environment to cope with them; (2) decisional control, concerning the access to various alternatives to deal with health-related issues, the ability to critically delve into them, and the willingness to be involved in making appropriate health deci-sions; (3) behavioral control, or the capacity to realize significant changes in everyday life behaviors, in order to act on the determinants of the individual psycho-physical well-being; (4) emotional regulation, which involves the capability to manage the stress associated with the illness and to enhance individual self-efficacy perception; and (5) hope for the future, that is to say the adoption of an optimistic attitude in dealing with impaired health conditions. In line with this conceptual framework, Barr et al. (2015) argued that three key domains are at the basis of the patient empowerment construct: (1) the states, experiences and capacities of the patients; (2) their actions and behaviors; and (3) their self-determination.

Scholars have also emphasized the role of information technologies and digital tools in facilitating the patient-provider relationship and encouraging the patients to actively participate in co-planning, co-designing, and co-delivering health services (Calvillo, Rom, & Roa, 2015). First of all, the use of information and communi-cation technologies for the purpose of health protection and promotion allow a deep redesign of the healthcare delivery system, in a perspective of increased patient-centeredness (Demiris et al., 2008; Fieschi, 2002). Besides, digital tools contribute in shrinking the barriers to patient empowerment (Safran, 2003), even though they raise several concerns about equity, mainly due to the problems associated with digital divide (Mackert, Mabry-Flynn, Champlin, Donovan, & Pounders 2016).

What is even more interesting, is that information and communication technologies contribute in increasing the processing abilities of the patients. Simultaneously, they could set the conditions for a more direct and genuine partnership between the patients and the healthcare professionals, thus fostering the process of patient empowerment (Wald, Dube, & Anthony, 2007). Last but not least, information technologies are crucial to promote the active participation of the patients in the design of health services, as well as their involvement in value co-creation processes (Grando, Rozenblum, & Bates, 2015). Among others, social networking and more direct communication exchanges between the healthcare providers and the patients have been argued to pave the way for greater opportunities of collaboration and health services' co-production (Eysenbach, 2008).

In line with these arguments, Umar and Mundy (2015) proposed an integrated model of patient empowerment, which relies, by the side of the healthcare providers, on the shift toward a patient-centered approach to care and, by the side of patients, on the enabling role of information and communication technologies. Digital tools and information technologies are considered to perform as an overarching infrastructure, which enacts an iterative process of activation and enhancement of the patients' sleeping resources. Going more into details, information technologies improve the ability of the patients to obtain, process, understand and use health information (Crook, Stephens, Pastorek, Mackert, & Donovan, 2016), and increase their willingness to be actively engaged in the provision of care, creating a supportive and shame-free environment, which encourages the patients to partner with the healthcare professionals to co-create value (Fortney, Burgess, Bosworth, Booth, & Kaboli, 2011).

Figure 1.3 provides a synoptic view of the ingredients which are required in the recipe for patient empowerment. Obviously, these ingredients are contributed by both the patients and the healthcare professionals. The former should be able and willing to actively participate in the provision of care. In other words, they should develop adequate knowledge, skills and attitudes to perform as value co-creators. In addition, they should increase their self-efficacy and self-determination, in order to be effectively involved in shared decision making. In turn, the healthcare professionals should concur in empowering the patients by embracing a patient-centered approach to care, which entails a focus on the patients' specific health needs, rather than on the illness. In addition, they should perform as catalysts, who activate the patients' sleeping resources and encourage them to be involved in the design and delivery of care. Information and communication technologies foster the process of patient empowerment. For this reason, they are represented as the pot which could be used to implement patient empowerment initiatives. Digital tools and information technologies boost patient empowerment, promoting the establishment of a more direct link between the patients and the healthcare professionals and curbing the barriers to the enablement of the patients' sleeping resources.

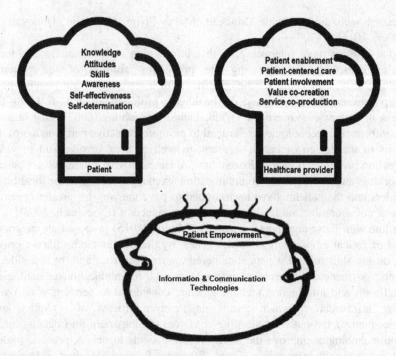

Fig. 1.3 A recipe for patient empowerment. *Source* Author's elaboration

1.5   Empowering Healthcare Organizations to Empower Patients

Scholars interested in patient empowerment initiatives have focused most their attention on the one-to-one patient-provider relationship, pointing out that personalization of health services, access to care, commitment to value co-creation, and therapeutic alliance could be considered as the building blocks of patient empowerment (Higgins, Larson, & Schnall, 2016). Alternatively, the ability of healthcare organizations to build an empowering environment, which encourages the involvement of patients in health services' co-production has been widely overlooked (Willis et al., 2014). This is striking, since the healthcare organizations host most of the interactions between the patients and the healthcare professionals (Annarumma & Palumbo, 2016). As a consequence, still little is known about the contribution of healthcare organizations in the process of patient empowerment. Nonetheless, there is a growing awareness of the important role played by the healthcare organizations in enabling the patients and engaging them in the provision of health services (Parker & Hernandez, 2012).

To delve into this issue, the "organizational health literacy" concept has been introduced in the scientific literature (Brach et al., 2012). Ultimately, it indicates the ability of healthcare organizations to establish a comfortable relationship with the patients, which facilitates the process of patient empowerment (Palumbo, 2016b). In fact, health literate healthcare organizations have been claimed to be more supportive of patient involvement interventions. They contribute in raising the patients' awareness of their crucial role in the healthcare delivery system and concur in the patient enabling process, activating the sleeping resources of the latter for the purpose of health protection and promotion (Livaudais-Toman et al., 2014). From this point of view, inadequate organizational health literacy could be depicted as one of the most relevant barriers to the implementation of service co-production in the healthcare environment (Palumbo, 2016b).

Sticking to these considerations, Koh, Brach, Harris, & Parchman, (2013) proposed a health literate healthcare model, which is claimed to rely on the ability of the healthcare organizations to assist the patients in accessing health-related resources and in properly using them to cope with their impaired health conditions. The greater the organizational health literacy, the more friendly and comfortable the relationship between the patients and the healthcare professionals and, consequently, the stronger the patients' willingness to be involved in self-management of care, shared decision making, co-design of health services, and value co-creation. In other words, the adoption of an organizational health literacy approach creates a favorable environment for patient empowerment and sets the condition for the active involvement of the latter in the provision of care. Obviously, a process intended to empower healthcare organizations is required, in order to make the latter able to assist the patients in performing as value co-creators in the healthcare service system (Hernandez, 2012).

Delving into this issue, Brach et al. (2012) suggested ten attributes of health literate healthcare organizations: they are understood as a set of distinguishing characteristics that make healthcare organizations capable to enlace a therapeutic alliance with the patients and to engage them as partners in the protection and promotion of individual well-being. In particular, health literate healthcare organizations are argued to: (1) rely on a group of leaders who make health literacy integral to organizational mission, structures, and operations; (2) contemplate health literacy in managerial processes, including planning, evaluation measures, patient safety initiatives, and quality improvement interventions; (3) prepare the healthcare providers to handle health literacy issues, raising the individual and collective awareness of the negative effects of inadequate health literacy on health outcomes; (4) engage the population served in the design, implementation, and evaluation of health services; (5) meet the needs of underserved population, overcoming stigma and shame associated with limited health literacy; (6) use tailored health literacy strategies in interpersonal communications and confirm the patients' understanding at all points of contact with them; (7) provide the patients and the informal caregivers with easy-to-access and easy-to-understand health information, assisting them in navigating the healthcare environment; (8) design and distribute print and audio-visual materials, as well as social media contents that are easy-to-understand; (9) provide support to the patients in high-risk situations, including care transitions and communications about medicines; and (10) communicate clearly what kind of services are covered by health plans and what kind of services should be paid out-of-pocket.

Table 1.1 summarizes the attributes of health literate healthcare organizations, attaching to each of them a brief description. Besides, it points out their contribution of organizational health literacy to the process of patient empowerment. In particular, the enhancement of organizational health literacy could be understood as a catalyst to the effectiveness of patient empowerment initiatives: health literate.

Table 1.1 The contribution of organizational health literacy (OHL) to patient empowerment (PE)

OHL attribute	Description	Contribution to PE
Supportive leadership	The leadership is aware of organizational health literacy and makes health literacy integral to its mission, structure, and operations	OHL is understood as a strategic priority, encouraging healthcare providers to engage patients in health services' delivery
OHL commitment	A specific health literacy concern is included into planning, evaluation measures, patient safety, and quality improvement	The health literate healthcare organization strives for enabling patients to have a role in value co-creation
Workforce training	Healthcare professionals are trained to be health literate and aware of health literacy-related issues	Healthcare providers are aware of the special needs of low health literate patients, empowering them
Population involvement	Users are engaged in designing, delivering, implementing, and evaluating health information and services	Patients are encouraged to be fully involved in the provision of care and in value co-creation
Organizational responsiveness	A range of organizational health literacy skills is available to meet the needs of the population served, avoiding stigma and shame	The health literate healthcare organization is able to activate the sleeping resources of patients, promoting their involvement in service co-production
Organizational friendliness	Tailored health literacy strategies are used at all points of contact with patients	Patients are empowered by facilitating their interactions with the healthcare professionals
Clear communication	Patients are provided with easy access to health information and services and navigation assistance	Patients are able to access timely and relevant information to actively participate in the provision of care
Effective communication	Patients are provided with print, audio-visual, and social media content that is easy to understand and act on	Patients are supported in dealing with health information, in order to properly function within the healthcare environment
Organizational readiness	Healthcare providers are able to address health literacy-related issues in high-risk situations, such as care transitions	Patients are empowered and encouraged to co-create value during the entire healthcare path
Organizational transparency	Patients are well informed about co-payments and charges	Patients are aware of the costs attached to different health choices

Source Author's adaptation from Brach et al. (2012)

healthcare organizations show a better ability to help the patients in navigating the healthcare service system, thus increasing their commitment to health services' co-production as well as to value co-creation.

In sum, organizational health literacy concurs in setting the conditions for the establishment of a partnership between the patients and the healthcare professionals. A poor health literate healthcare environment produces a disempowering effect on patients, discouraging them to be involved in the provision of care (Annarumma & Palumbo, 2016). It is worth noting that the ability of healthcare organizations to address health literacy-related issues has been found to be critical in a perspective of health services' quality improvement (Mabachi et al., 2016). From this point of view, the empowerment of healthcare organizations could be argued to be crucial in order to empower patients and to stimulate their willingness to be engaged in health services' delivery. Among others, healthcare professionals play a significant role in realizing such a process of organizational empowerment (Brach, Dreyer, & Schillinger, 2014). Indeed, they are able to influence the organizational health literacy attributes of healthcare organizations, thus improving their ability to build a therapeutic alliance with the patients.

1.6 Realizing the Potential of Patient Empowerment: An Overview

Patient empowerment is a multifaceted concept, which brings toward a new model of healthcare provision. Indeed, it is consistent with a patient-centered approach to care, which focuses on the health needs of patients rather than on illnesses and health treatments. From this point of view, patient empowerment could be conceptualized as a practice of freedom, which is intended to increase the ability and the willingness of patients to perform as partners of healthcare providers in the delivery of health services.

Since it relies on the patient-provider relationship, patient empowerment could be better understood by embracing a relational perspective. Both the patients and the healthcare providers participate in realizing the full potential of patient empowerment. On the one hand, the patients have to develop the knowledge, the skills and the attitudes which are required to properly function within the healthcare service system; moreover, they should be aware of their role in the process of value co-creation, accepting to establish a therapeutic alliance with the providers of care. On the other hand, healthcare professionals should dismiss their loyalty to the traditional biomedical model, performing as enablers of the patients' sleeping resources. In other words, rather than sticking to a mere fix-it approach, they should strive for engaging the patients in the promotion and protection of their psycho-physical well-being, involving them in co-planning, co-designing and co-delivering health services.

Drawing on these arguments, patient empowerment should be conceived as both a process and an outcome. In fact, it is rooted in the patient-provider relationship, which is reframed around the purposes of enabling, activating, engaging and involving the patients. At the same time, it results in an innovative model of healthcare provision, which understands the patients as key value co-creators, rather than as sheer consumers of professional-led health services.

Information and communication technologies are expected to foster the process of patient empowerment, disintermediating the relationship between the healthcare providers and the patients and improving the processing skills of the latter. Moreover, digital tools contribute in removing the barriers to patient empowerment, creating a shame-free environment which encourages the patients to be actively involved in the healthcare delivery system as value co-creators.

In spite of these considerations, it is interesting to note that the healthcare organizations still represent the setting which hosts most of the interactions between the patients and the healthcare professionals. Therefore, the enhancement of the healthcare organizations' ability to establish a friendly and comfortable relationship with the patients turns out to be crucial to realize the full potential of patient empowerment interventions. Among others, the improvement of organizational health literacy is expected to set the conditions for the establishment of a long-term co-creating partnership between the patients and the healthcare professionals, paving the way for patient empowerment.

References

Adinolfi, P. (2014). Philosophy, medicine and healthcare: Insights from the Italian experience. *Health Care Analysis, 22*(3), 223–244.

Adinolfi, P., Starace, F., & Palumbo, R. (2016). Health outcomes and patient empowerment. The case of health budgets in Italy. *Journal of Health Management, 18*(1), 117–133.

Alexa, J., Recka, L., Votápková, J., van Ginneken, E., Spranger, A., & Wittenbecher, F. (2015). Czech republic: Health system review. *Health Systems in Transition, 7*(1), 1–165.

Anderson, R. M., & Funnell, M. M. (2005). Patient empowerment: reflections on the challenge of fostering the adoption of a new paradigm. *Patient Education and Counseling, 57*(2), 153–157.

Anderson, R. M., & Funnell, M. M. (2010). Patient empowerment: Myths and misconceptions. *Patient Education and Counseling, 79*(3), 277–282.

Anell, A., Glenngård, A. H., & Merkur, S. (2012). Sweden: Health system review. *Health Systems in Transition, 14*(5), 1–159.

Annarumma, C., & Palumbo, R. (2016). Contextualizing health literacy to health care organizations: Exploratory insights. *Journal of Health Management, 18*(4), 611–624.

Ashcroft, R., & Van Katwyk, T. (2016). An Examination of the biomedical paradigm: A view of social work. *Social Work in Public Health, 31*(3), 140–152.

Asimakopoulou, K., Gilbert, D., Newton, P., & Scambler, S. (2012). Back to basics: Re-examining the role of patient empowerment in diabetes. *Patient Education and Counseling, 86*(3), 281–283.

Aujoulat, I., d'Hoore, W., & Deccache, A. (2007). Patient empowerment in theory and practice: Polysemy or cacophony? *Patient Education and Counseling, 66*(1), 13–20.

Aujoulat, I., Marcolongo, R., Bonadiman, L., & Deccache, A. (2008). Reconsidering patient empowerment in chronic illness: A critique of models of self-efficacy and bodily control. *Social Science and Medicine, 66*(5), 1228–1239.

Barr, P. J., Scholl, I., Bravo, P., Faber, M. J., Elwyn, G., & McAllister, M. (2015). Assessment of patient empowerment—A systematic review of measures. *PLoS ONE, 10*(5), e0126553.

Barros, P., Machado, S., & Simões, J. (2011). Portugal: Health system review. *Health Systems in Transition, 13*(4), 1–156.

Barry, M. J., & Edgman-Levitan, S. (2012). Shared decision making—The pinnacle of patient-centered care. *New England Journal of Medicine, 366*(9), 780–781.

Bauman, A. E., Fardy, H. J., & Harris, P. G. (2003). Getting it right: Why bother with patient-centred care? *Medical Journal of Australia, 179*(5), 253–256.

Bechtel, C., & Ness, D. L. (2010). If you build it, will they come? Designing truly patient-centered health care. *Health Affairs, 29*(5), 914–920.

Bella, L. (2010). In sickness and in health: Public and private responsibility for health care from Bismarck to Obama. In R. Harris, N. Wathen, & S. Wyatt (Eds.), *Configuring health consumers: Health work and the imperative of personal responsibility* (pp. 13–29). London: Palgrave Macmillan.

Bennett, C. C. (2013). Are we there yet? A journey of health reform in Australia. *Medical Journal of Australia, 199*(4), 251–255.

Bernabeo, E., & Holmboe, E. S. (2013). Patients, providers, and systems need to acquire a specific set of competencies to achieve truly patient-centered care. *Health Affairs, 32*(2), 250–258.

Bertakis, K. D., & Azari, R. (2011). Determinants and outcomes of patient-centered care. *Patient Education and Counseling, 85*(1), 46–52.

Brach, C., Dreyer, B. P., & Schillinger, D. (2014). Physicians' roles in creating health literate organizations: A call to action. *Journal of General Internal Medicine, 29*(2), 273–275.

Brach, C., Keller, D., Hernandez, L. M., Baur, C., Parker, R., Dreyer, B., et al. (2012). *Ten attributes of health literate health care organizations*. Washington DC: Institute of Medicine.

Bravo, P., Edwards, A., Barr, P. J., Scholl, I., Elwyn, G., & McAllister, M. (2015). Conceptualising patient empowerment: A mixed methods study. *BMC Health Services Research, 15*(1), 252.

Busse, R., & Blümel, M. (2014). Germany: Health system review. *Health Systems in Transition, 16*(2), 1–296.

Callahan, L. F., & Pincus, T. (1997). Education, self-care, and diseases: Further challenges to the "Biomedical Model" outcomes of rheumatic paradigm. *Arthritis and Rheumatism, 10*(5), 283–288.

Calvillo, J., Rom, I., & Roa, L. M. (2015). How technology is empowering patients? A literature review. *Health Expectations, 18*(5), 643–652.

Canadian Council on Learning. (2007). *Health literacy in Canada: Initial results from the international adult literacy and skills survey*. Ottawa: Canadian Council on Literacy.

Chatzimarkakis, J. (2010). Why patients should be more empowered: A European perspective on lessons learned in the management of diabetes. *Journal of Diabetes Science and Technology, 4*(6), 1570–1573.

Chevreul, K., Berg Brigham, K., Durand-Zaleski, I., & Hernández-Quevedo, C. (2015). France: Health system review. *Health Systems in Transition, 17*(3), 1–218.

Chiauzzi, E., DasMahapatra, P., Cochin, E., Bunce, M., Khoury, R., & Dave, P. (2016). Factors in patient empowerment: A survey of an online patient research network. *The Patient, 9*(6), 511–523.

Clancy, C. M. (2011). Patient engagement in health care. *Health Services Research, 46*(2), 389–393.

Colombo, C., Moja, L., Gonzalez-Lorenzo, M., Liberati, A., & Mosconi, P. (2012). Patient empowerment as a component of health system reforms: rights, benefits and vested interests. *Internal and Emergency Medicine, 7*(2), 183–187.

Crook, B., Stephens, K. K., Pastorek, A. E., Mackert, M., & Donovan, E. E. (2016). Sharing health information and influencing behavioral intentions: The role of health literacy, information overload, and the internet in the diffusion of healthy heart information. *Health Communication, 31*(1), 60–71.

Cylus, J., Richardson, E., Findley, L., Longley, M., O'Neill, C., & Steel, D. (2015). United Kingdom: Health system review. *Health Systems in Transition, 17*(5), 1–125.

de Boer, D., Delnoij, D., & Rademakers, J. (2013). The importance of patient-centered care for various patient groups. *Patient Education and Counseling, 90*(3), 405–410.

Demiris, G., Afrin, L. B., Speedie, S., Courtney, K. L., Sondhi, M., Vimarlund, V., et al. (2008). Patient-centered applications: Use of information technology to promote disease management and wellness. A white paper by the AMIA knowledge in motion working group. *Journal of the American Medical Informatics Association, 15*(1), 8–13.

Distiller, L. A., Brown, M. A., Joffe, B. I., & Kramer, B. D. (2010). Striving for the impossible dream: A community-based multi-practice collaborative model of diabetes management. *Diabetic Medicine, 27*(2), 197–202.

Dowling, M., Murphy, K., Cooney, A., & Casey, D. (2011). A concept analysis of empowerment in chronic illness from the perspective of the nurse and the client living with chronic obstructive pulmonary disease. *Journal of Nursing and Healthcare Chronic Illness, 3*(4), 476–487.

Džakula, A., Sagan, A., Pavić, N., Lončarek, K., & Sekelj-Kauzlarić, K. (2014). Croatia: Health system review. *Health Systems in Transition, 16*(3), 1–162.

Economou, C. (2010). Greece: Health system review. *Health Systems in Transition, 12*(7), 1–180.

Ekman, I., Swedberg, K., Taft, C., Lindseth, A., Norberg, A., Brink, E., et al. (2011). Person-centered care—Ready for prime time. *European Journal of Cardiovascular Nursing, 10,* 248–251.

Elwyn, G., Edwards, A., & Thompson, R. (2016). *Shared decision making in health care: Achieving evidence-based patient choice.* Oxford: Oxford University Press.

Engel, G. L. (1989). The need for a new medical model: A challenge for biomedicine. *Holistic Medicine, 4*(1), 37–53.

Epstein, R. M., & Street, R. L., Jr. (2011). The values and value of patient-centered care. *Annals of Family Medicine, 9*(2), 100–103.

Eysenbach, G. (2008). Medicine 2.0: Social networking, collaboration, participation, apomediation, and openness. *Journal of Medical Internet Research, 10*(3), e22.

Ferré, F., de Belvis, A. G., Valerio, L., Longhi, S., Lazzari, A., Fattore, G., et al. (2014). Italy: Health system review. *Health Systems in Transition, 16*(4), 1–168.

Fieschi, M. (2002). Information technology is changing the way society sees health care delivery. *International Journal of Medical Informatics, 66*(1–3), 85–93.

Fortney, J., Burgess, J., Jr., Bosworth, H., Booth, B., & Kaboli, P. (2011). A re-conceptualization of access for 21st century healthcare. *Journal of General Internal Medicine, 26*(2), 639–647.

Freidson, E. (1970). *Professional dominance: The social structure of medical care.* New York, USA: Atherton Press.

Fumagalli, L. P., Radaelli, G., Lettieri, E., Bertele', P., & Masella, C. (2015). Patient empowerment and its neighbours: Clarifying the boundaries and their mutual relationships. *Health Policy, 119*(3), 384–394.

Funnell, M. M., & Anderson, R. M. (2004). Empowerment and self-management of diabetes. *Clinical Diabetes, 22*(3), 123–127.

Funnell, M. M., Anderson, R. M., Arnold, M. S., Barr, P. A., Donnelly, M., Johnson, P. D., et al. (1991). Empowerment: An idea whose time has come in diabetes education. *The Diabetes Educator, 17*(1), 37–41.

Gachoud, D., Albert, M., Kuper, A., Stroud, L., & Reeves, S. (2012). Meanings and perceptions of patient-centeredness in social work, nursing and medicine: A comparative study. *Journal of Interprofessional Care, 26*(6), 484–490.

García-Armesto, S., Abadía-Taira, M. B., Durán, A., Hernández-Quevedo, C., & Bernal-Delgado, E. (2010). Spain: Health system review. *Health Systems in Transition, 12*(4), 1–295.

Gerkens, S., & Merkur, S. (2010). Belgium: Health system review. *Health Systems in Transition, 12*(5), 1–266.

Grando, M. A., Rozenblum, R., & Bates, D. (2015). *Information technology for patient empowerment in healthcare.* Berlin: Walter de Gruyter.

Gruman, J., Rovner, M. H., French, M. E., Jeffress, D., Sofaer, S., Shaller, D., et al. (2010). From patient education to patient engagement: Implications for the field of patient education. *Patient Education and Counseling, 78*(3), 350–356.

Hain, D., & Dianne, S. (2013). Partners in care: Patient empowerment through shared decision-making. *Nephrology Nursing Journal, 40*(2), 153–157.

Healy, J., Sharman, E., & Lokuge, B. (2006). Australia: Health system review. *Health Systems in Transition, 8*(5), 1–158.

Hernandez, L. M. (2012). *How can health care organizations become more health literate?: Workshop summary.* Washington DC: The National Academy Press.

Hibbard, J. H., & Greene, J. (2013). What the evidence shows about patient activation: Better health outcomes and care experiences. Fewer data on costs. *Health Affairs, 32*(2), 207–214.

Hibbard, J. H., Mahoney, E. R., Stock, R., & Tusler, M. (2007). Do increases in patient activation result in improved self-management behaviors? *Health Services Research, 42*(4), 1443–1463.

Higgins, T., Larson, E., & Schnall, R. (2016). Unraveling the meaning of patient engagement: A concept analysis. *Patient Education and Counseling, 100*(1), 30–36.

Holmström, I., & Röing, M. (2010). The relation between patient-centeredness and patient empowerment: A discussion on concepts. *Patient Education and Counseling, 79*(2), 167–172.

Huckman, R. S., & Kelley, M. A. (2013). Public reporting, consumerism, and patient empowerment. *New England Journal of Medicine, 369*(20), 1875–1877.

Jilka, S. R., Callahan, R., Sevdalis, N., Mayer, E. K., & Darzi, A. (2015). "Nothing about me without me": An interpretative review of patient accessible electronic health records. *Journal of Medical Internet Research, 17*(6), e161.

Johnson, M. O., Rose, C. D., Dilworth, S. E., & Neilands, T. B. (2012). Advances in the conceptualization and measurement of health care development and validation of the health care empowerment inventory. *PLoS One, 7*(9), e45692.

Jones, I. R., Berney, L., Kelly, M., Doyal, L., Griffiths, C., Feder, G., et al. (2004). Is patient involvement possible when decisions involve scarce resources? A qualitative study of decision-making in primary care. *Social Science and Medicine, 59*(1), 93–102.

Kaldoudi, E., & Makris, N. (2015). Patient Empowerment as a Cognitive Process. In C. Verdier, M. Bienkiewicz, A. Fred, H. Gamboa, & D. Elias (Eds.), *8th international conference on health informatics* (pp. 605–610). Portugal: Lisbon.

Koh, H. K., Brach, C., Harris, L. M., & Parchman, M. L. (2013). A proposed 'Health literate care model' would constitute a systems approach to improving patients' engagement in care. *Health Affairs, 32*(2), 357–367.

Kroneman, M., Boerma, W., van den Berg, M., Groenewegen, P., de Jong, J., & van Ginneken, E. (2016). The Netherlands: Health system review. *Health Systems in Transition, 18*(2), 1–239.

Livaudais-Toman, J., Burke, N. J., Napoles, A., & Kaplan, C. P. (2014). Health literate organizations: Are clinical trial sites equipped to recruit minority and limited health literacy patients? *Journal of Health Disparities Research and Practice, 7*(4), 1–13.

Longino, C. F., & Murphy, J. W. (1995). *The old age challenge to the biomedical model: Paradigm strain and health policy.* London: Routledge.

Mabachi, N. M., Cifuentes, M., Barnard, J., Brega, A. G., Albright, K., Weiss, B. D., et al. (2016). Demonstration of the health literacy universal precautions toolkit: Lessons for quality improvement. *Journal of Ambulatory Care Management, 39*(3), 199–208.

Mackert, M., Mabry-Flynn, A., Champlin, S., Donovan, E. E., & Pounders, K. (2016). Health literacy and health information technology adoption: The potential for a new digital divide. *Journal of Medical Internet Research, 18*(10), e264.

Marchildon, G. P. (2013). Canada: Health system review. *Health Systems in Transition, 15*(1), 1–179.

McAllister, M., Dunn, G., Payne, K., Davies, L., & Todd, C. (2012). Patient empowerment: The need to consider it as a measurable patient-reported outcome for chronic conditions. *BMC Health Services Research, 12*(1), 157. doi:10.1186/1472-6963-12-157.

McGuckin, M., & Govednik, J. (2014). Patient empowerment begins with knowledge: Consumer perceptions and knowledge sources for hand hygiene compliance rates. *American Journal of Infection Control, 42*(10), 1106–1108.

Mead, N., Bower, P., & Roland, M. (2008). Factors associated with enablement in general practice: Cross-sectional study using routinely-collected data. *British Journal of General Practice, 58*(550), 346–352.

Mitenbergs, U., Taube, M., Misins, J., Mikitis, E., Martinsons, A., Rurane, A., et al. (2012). Latvia: Health system review. *Health Systems in Transition, 14*(8), 1–191.

Olejaz, M., Juul Nielsen, A., Rudkjøbing, A., Okkels Birk, H., Krasnik, A., & Hernández-Quevedo, C. (2012). Denmark: Health system review. *Health Systems in Transition*, 1–192.

Palumbo, R. (2016a). Contextualizing co-production of health care: A systematic literature review. *International Journal of Public Sector Management, 29*(1), 72–90.

Palumbo, R. (2016b). Designing health-literate health care organization: A literature review. *Health Services Management Research, 29*(3), 79–87.

Parker, R. M., & Hernandez, L. M. (2012). What makes an organization health literate? *Journal of Health Communication, 17*(5), 624–627.

Pawlikowska, T., Zhang, W., Griffiths, F., van Dalen, J., & van der Vleuten, C. (2012). Verbal and non-verbal behavior of doctors and patients in primary care consultations—How this relates to patient enablement. *Patient Education and Counseling, 86*(1), 70–76.

Pelletier, L. R., & Stichler, J. F. (2013). Action brief: Patient engagement and activation: A health reform imperative and improvement opportunity for nursing. *Nursing Outlook, 61*(1), 51–54.

Piper, S. (2010). Patient empowerment: Emancipatory or technological practice? *Patient Education and Counseling, 79*(2), 173–177.

Prigge, J.-K., Dietz, B., Homburg, C., Hoyer, W. D., & Burton, J. L. (2015). Patient empowerment: A cross-disease exploration of antecedents and consequences. *International Journal of Research in Marketing, 32*(4), 375–386.

Rappaport, J. (1987). Terms of empowerment/exemplars of prevention: Toward a theory for community psychology. *American Journal of Community Psychology, 15*(2), 121–144.

Rathert, C., Wyrwich, M. D., & Boren, S. A. (2013). Patient-centered care and outcomes. A systematic review of the literature. *Medical Care Research and Review, 70*(4), 351–379.

Rice, T., Rosenau, P., Unruh, L. Y., Barnes, A. J., Saltman, R. B., & van Ginneken, E. (2013). United States of America. *Health Systems in Transition, 15*(3), 1–431.

Ringard, Å., Sagan, A., Sperre Saunes, I., & Lindahl, A. K. (2013). Norway: Health system review. *Health Systems in Transition, 15*(8), 1–162.

Roberts, K. J. (1999). Patient empowerment in the United States: A critical commentary. *Health Expectations, 2*(2), 82–92.

Rowland, K. J., & Politi, M. C. (2016). Shared decision-making and the patient-provider relationship. In M. A. Diefenbach, S. Miller-Halegoua, & D. J. Bowen (Eds.), *Handbook of health decision science* (pp. 181–192). New York: Springer.

Safran, C. (2003). The collaborative edge: Patient empowerment for vulnerable populations. *International Journal of Medical Informatics, 69*(2–3), 185–190.

Salmon, P., & Hall, G. M. (2003). Patient empowerment and control: A psychological discourse in the service of medicine. *Social Science and Medicine, 57*(10), 1969–1980.

Segal, L. (1998). The importance of patient empowerment in health system reform. *Health Policy, 44*(1), 31–44.

Simpson, D. D. (2004). A conceptual framework for drug treatment process and outcomes. *Journal of Substance Abuse Treatment, 27*(2), 99–121.

Small, N., Bower, P., Chew-Graham, C. A., Whalley, D., & Protheroe, J. (2013). Patient empowerment in long-term conditions: Development and preliminary testing of a new measure. *BMC Health Services Research, 13*(1), 263. doi:10.1186/1472-6963-13-263.

Sminkey, P. V. (2013). Patient empowerment and health care reform. *Professional Case Management, 18*(6), 325–327.

The Lancet. (2012). Patient empowerment—Who empowers whom? *Lancet, 379*(9827), 1677.

Thompson, A. G. (2007). The meaning of patient involvement and participation in health care consultations: A taxonomy. *Social Science and Medicine, 64*(6), 1297–1310.

Topac, V., & Stoicu-Tivadar, V. (2013). Patient empowerment by increasing the understanding of medical language for lay users. *Methods of Information in Medicine, 52*(5), 454–462.

Umar, A., & Mundy, D. (2015). Re-thinking models of patient empowerment. *Study in Health Technology and Informatics, 209*, 175–181.

van de Bovenkamp, H. M., & Trappenburg, M. J. (2009). Reconsidering patient participation in guideline development. *Health Care Analysis, 17*(3), 198–216.

Vlădescu, C., Scîntee, S. G., Olsavszky, V., Hernández-Quevedo, C., & Sagan, A. (2016). Romania: Health system review. *Health Systems in Transition, 18*(4), 1–170.

Vuorenkoski, L., Mladovsky, P., & Mossialos, E. (2008). Finland: Health system review. *Health Systems in Transition, 10*(4), 1–168.

Wald, H. S., Dube, C. E., & Anthony, D. C. (2007). Untangling the web—The impact of Internet use on health care and the physician–patient relationship. *Patient Education and Counseling, 68*(3), 218–224.

Wan, C. R., Vo, L., & Barnes, C. S. (2012). Conceptualizations of patient empowerment among individuals seeking treatment for diabetes mellitus in an urban, public-sector clinic. *Patient Education and Counseling, 87*(3), 402–404.

Whitehead, M., Hanratty, B., & Popay, J. (2010). NHS reform: Untried remedies for misdiagnosed problems? *Health Affairs, 376*(9750), 1373–1375.

Williams, G. C. (2002). Improving patients' health through supporting the autonomy of patients and providers. In E. L. Deci & R. M. Ryan (Eds.), *Handbook of self-determination research* (pp. 233–254). Rochester: The University of Rochester Press.

Willis, C., Saul, J., Bitz, J., Pompu, K., Best, A., & Jackson, B. (2014). Improving organizational capacity to address health literacy in public health: A rapid realist review. *Public Health, 128* (6), 515–524.

Wilson, H. J. (2000). The myth of objectivity: Is medicine moving towards a social constructivist medical paradigm? *Family Practice, 17*(2), 203–209.

Wilson, P. M. (2001). A policy analysis of the Expert Patient in the United Kingdom: Self-care as an expression of pastoral power? *Health and Social Care, 9*(3), 134–142.

Chapter 2
The Bright Side of Patient Empowerment

2.1 Patients as Value Co-creators

As argued in the previous section, empowerment could be conceptualized as a practice of freedom (Freire, 1993). When this concept is applied to the experience of patients in the healthcare environment, empowerment is better understood if a relational perspective is adopted (Tang, Funnell, Brown, & Kurlander, 2010). Going more into details, patient empowerment relies on the establishment of a co-creating partnership between the patients and the healthcare professionals: the former accept to actively participate in the design and delivery of care, while the latter perform as enablers of the patients' sleeping resources. Therefore, it could be maintained that value co-creation is a distinguishing attribute of patient empowerment initiatives. Indeed, patient empowerment paves the way for a process of enablement, which is aimed at encouraging patient involvement in shared decision making (Hardyman, Daunt, & Kitchener, 2015). However, it is difficult to provide a comprehensive definition of value and value co-creation in the healthcare service system.

Scholars have widely discussed the meaning and measurement of value in healthcare, claiming the multidimensionality of this concept (Porter, 2010). Different concerns have been raised in the attempt to define the different shades of value in the healthcare environment, including the need to account for: health outcomes, safety, quality, cost, equity and innovation (Yong, Olsen, & McGinnis, 2010). The idea of patient-centered value is gradually emerging as a glue which is able to bind together these various definition of value, synthesizing them (Rollow & Cucchiara, 2016). Moreover, it is worth noting that such a patient-centered interpretation of value is consistent with patient engagement in health protection and health promotion activities.

The value co-creation concept is not odd in the scientific literature (Prahalad & Ramaswamy, 2004). Ultimately, it relies on the assumption that the healthcare professionals and the patients—rather than sticking to a relieving approach,

© The Author(s) 2017

P. Rocco, *The Bright Side and the Dark Side of Patient Empowerment*,
SpringerBriefs in Public Health, DOI 10.1007/978-3-319-58344-0_2 .

according to which the providers of care perform as the sole value creators and the patients as mere consumers of health services—have the opportunity to join their efforts, in order to create a unique value, which is worth for both the parties (Vargo & Lusch, 2008). The link between patient-centered care and value co-creation is evident: in fact, patient-centered care inspires a thorough reconceptualization of patients as service co-producers (Moll, 2010), leading toward a shared approach to care (Pritchard & Hughes, 1995).

Drawing on these considerations, scholars are paying a growing attention to value co-creation in the healthcare service system. In particular, patient involvement in the delivery of care has been argued to be crucial to: improve the quality of health services, increase the effectiveness of care, enhance health outcomes and save available resources (Pinho, Beirão, Patrício, & Fisk, 2014). From this point of view, patient involvement is able to match the multidimensionality of value concepts in the healthcare environment. Also, Elg, Engström, Witell, and Poksinska (2012) emphasized that value co-creation could be beneficial for the healthcare providers themselves: they have the opportunity to learn from the patients, who provide relevant insights to improve professional practices. This is possible by generating and collecting the patients' ideas to realize the full potential of patient-centered care and further encourage patient involvement.

Sticking to these arguments, it has been claimed that value co-creation is inherent in the patient-provider relationship (Palumbo, 2015). Nonetheless, a process of empowerment is required in order to raise the awareness of the positive consequences which could be attached to patient involvement, as well as to assist both the patients and the healthcare professionals to establish an effective co-creating partnership (Davis, Jacklin, Sevdalis, & Vincent, 2007). As depicted in Chap. 1, healthcare organizations themselves play an important role in promoting value co-creation. In fact, they are able to support collaborative patient-provider relationships, building an organizational culture which relies on openness and enhancing the ability of the staff to involve the patients in the delivery of care (Renedo, Marston, Spyridonidis, & Barlow, 2015).

Embracing this perspective and defining value co-creation as the "...*benefit realized from integration of resources through activities and interactions with collaborators in the customer's service network*", McColl-Kennedy, Vargo, Dagger, Sweeney, and van Kasteren (2012, p. 375) identified five recurring co-creation practice styles which could be applied to health services' design and delivery: (1) passive compliance, (2) pragmatic adapting, (3) partnering, (4) insular controlling, and (5) team management. As reported in Table 2.1, these styles are characterized by increasing levels of patients' participation and, consequently, by varying intensity of patient empowerment.

Passive compliance is characterized by a limited patient involvement in health decision making. The healthcare professionals maintain a significant control over the process of health services' design and delivery; however, patients are encouraged and supported in complying with medical prescriptions, as well as in following healthy life-styles, which help them in coping with their health-related conditions. Therefore, the providers of care do not participate in patient enablement

Table 2.1 Value co-creation styles and levels of patient empowerment

Value co-creation style	Description	Level of patient empowerment
Passive compliance	Patients' participation in the provision of care is limited. In most of the cases, the patients are provided with information and support to comply with medical prescriptions	Patient enablement aimed at improving therapeutic compliance
Pragmatic adapting	The patients are supported in coping with their health-related conditions, developing tailored self-care skills	Patient enablement and activation intended to increase the patients' self-care abilities
Partnering	The healthcare professionals and the patients enter in a co-creating relationships, where both of them contribute in value co-creation	Patient engagement
Insular controlling	The patients gain control over the process of healthcare delivery; they are involved in health decision making, but still rely on the enabling role of healthcare providers	Patient involvement and shared decision making
Team management	The patients are fully empowered and they perform as key actors in the process of value creation. The healthcare professionals stick to a patient-centered approach to care and support patient empowerment	Full-fledged patient empowerment

Source Author's adaptation from McColl-Kennedy et al. (2012)

initiatives which are intended to make the patients able to autonomously make health decisions. As a Consequence, the only contribution of the patients in value co-creation stands in medication adherence and therapeutic compliance.

Pragmatic adapting share several common traits with passive compliance, but it shows a limited activation of the patients for the purposes of health protection and promotion. In fact, the patients are encouraged to recognize and deal with their health status, in order to better adapt their every-day behaviors to the changed circumstances of life which are associated with the emergence of the disease. In this case, the healthcare providers perform as enablers and catalyzers of the patients' sleeping assets, inciting them to participate in the process of value co-creation. Notwithstanding, shared decision making is still limited.

Partnering involves the establishment of a therapeutic alliance between the patients and the healthcare professionals. In fact, the patients are engaged in designing and delivering health services, cooperating with the healthcare providers in order to effectively cope with the illness. Hence, the patients gain greater control over the process of value creation, being engaged in shared decision making. Obviously, patient engagement requires the development of adequate health-related knowledge, skills and attitudes by the side of patients. In this way, it is possible to enhance their self-efficacy perception and their willingness to perform as value co-creators. Beyond contributing to enable the assets of the patients, the healthcare professionals strive for encouraging patient engagement, in an attempt to collect from the patients as many insights as possible to improve the timeliness, quality and effectiveness of care.

Insular controlling and team management present the greatest intensity of value co-creation. On the one hand, the patients are involved in co-planning, co-designing and co-delivering health services, obtaining a relevant control over the process of value creation. However, they still rely on healthcare professionals, who lead the provision of care. On the other hand, the patients are able to balance the power of healthcare professionals during the medical encounter, being involved at all the stages of healthcare provision. In other words, insular controlling implies the engagement of the patients in health decision making, while team management involves a full-fledged process of patient empowerment, which is based on the establishment of a long-term partnership between the patients and the healthcare professionals and is consistent with a patient-centered approach to care.

Summarizing these considerations, a bidirectional relationship could be argued to link value co-creation styles and patient empowerment. To participate in value co-creation, the patients need to develop adequate knowledge, skills and attitudes, which are required to properly function in the healthcare service system. Patient empowerment allows to enable and activate the sleeping resources of patients, as well as to engage and involve them in the delivery of care. In turn, the participation of patients in value co-creation paves the way for a self-nourishing virtuous cycle of patient empowerment. The more the patients perform as value co-creators, the stronger their self-efficacy perception and, consequently, the higher their willingness to be involved in the appropriate functioning of the healthcare delivery system. From this point of view, patient empowerment and value co-creation could be understood as conjoined twins, which jointly contribute in the transition toward patient-centered care.

2.2 Patients as Service Co-producers

Service co-production is a popular concept in the field of public management (Osborne & Strokosch, 2013). In a quite similar way, it is attracting a growing attention among scholars interested in healthcare management and public health (Palumbo, 2016), where it is dealt with as an innovative approach to care which is intended to improve the overall functioning of the healthcare service system (Loeffler, Power, Bovaird, & Hine-Hughes, 2012). The idea of service co-production was introduced in late '70s, when Ostrom and Ostrom (1977) pointed out that users play a crucial role in the delivery of public services. Echoing this consideration, Sharp (1980) claimed that public services are always the joint products of providers and users. In particular, the users of public services have been argued to perform as prosumers, that is to say as both consumers and co-producers of public value (Whitaker, 1980; Parks et al., 1981; Riessman & Banks, 2001; Bovaird et al., 2015).

Both patient centeredness and patient empowerment are recurring concepts in the healthcare environment (Rathert, Wyrwich, & Boren, 2013). Ultimately, they imply a shift in the functioning of the healthcare delivery system (Mead & Bower, 2000), which is inspired by a deep reconceptualization of the patient-provider relationship (Dahlberg, 1996; McLaughlin, 2004). Such a shift aims at mitigating the conditions of psychological dependence and information asymmetry of the patient (Freidson, 1970). Actually, a participative care model is introduced (Guadagnoli & Ward, 1998), which recognizes the patients as the subjects—rather than the objects—of healthcare provision (Takman & Severinsson, 1999). From this standpoint, patient centeredness, patient empowerment and co-production of health services turn out to be strictly intertwined: they are intended to improve the quality of care, involving the patients in the protection and promotion of their health conditions and engaging them in a virtuous process of value co-creation (Cramm & Nieboer, 2015).

To involve the patients in the co-production of health services, the healthcare professionals should dismiss the traditional biomedical model to care, according to which the healthcare providers control the medical encounter focusing on the treatment of the illness (Saha, Beach, & Cooper, 2008). Rather, the patients are considered to perform as key partners of regular providers: they contribute in planning and implementing the provision of care, bringing in knowledge, resources, skills and specific information which are essential to design and deliver tailored and effective health services (Palumbo, 2016; Pomey, Ghadiri, Karazivan, Fernandez, & Clavel, 2015). What is even more interesting, is that the healthcare professionals could not benefit from the patients' sleeping assets if they do not strive for enabling and empowering them during the medical encounter, paying attention to the specific patients' health needs (see, among others: Bertakis & Azari, 2011; Cegala, Street, & Clinch, 2007; Weingart et al., 2011).

In sum, the co-production of health services relies on the assumption that the success of healthcare provision does not solely rely on the expertise of healthcare professionals and on their ability to properly diagnose the patients' health-related conditions, in order to arrange an appropriate treatment to cope with them (Bettencourt, Ostrom, Brown, & Roundtree, 2002). Quite the opposite, the participation of patients in self-managing their health conditions and their self-confidence in navigating the healthcare service system are considered to be fundamental ingredients of the recipe for a more effective and appropriate access to care (Needham, 2012).

From this standpoint, the medical encounter is reframed as a relationship between two experts, who jointly participate in the provision of care (Pawlikowska, Zhang, Griffiths, van Dalen, & van der Vleuten, 2012). On the one hand, the healthcare providers contributes in value co-creation with their professional knowledge and skills, which are required to devise a timely health treatment to meet the health needs of the patient. On the other hand, the patient contributes in value co-creation with both the information related to his or her own disease experience—which, in most of the cases, are tacit—as well as with the activation of the individual sleeping resources to effectively cope with the illness (Mattingly, Tom, Stuart, & Onukwugha, 2016; Murray & McCrone, 2015). Therefore, the medical encounter is not exclusively led by the healthcare professionals. Rather, it is understood as a co-creating partnership, during which the patients and the providers collaborate to co-plan, co-design and co-deliver a tailored and person-centered health treatment (Street, Makoul, Arora, & Epstein, 2009).

Scholars have suggested various taxonomies to shed light on the different approaches to public service co-production. Taking into consideration the breadth and depth of user engagement, Brudney and England (1983) identified three main types of service co-production. Collective co-production is aimed at involving the population served in planning public services, in order to enhance their responsiveness to the evolving needs of the community. In this case, service co-production broadly concerns the potential users of public services, who participate in planning and designing public services. However, the users are generally not allowed to participate in the process of service provision, which still relies on traditional providers (Bovaird, Van Ryzin, Loeffler, & Parrado, 2015; Weaver, 2011). As compared with collective co-production, group co-production shows a greater depth, but a more limited extent of user involvement. In fact, group co-production strives for empowering homogeneous groups of users who express common needs, engaging them in the delivery system, with the purpose of expanding the range of services provided and increasing their effectiveness (Tu, 2016). Lastly, individual co-production entails the establishment of a direct and co-creating relationship between the users and the providers (Wirth, 1991). It attempts to stress the users' role in the process of value co-creation, involving them as active partners in service design and delivery. Hence, this co-production style is deeper, but narrower as compared with both collective and group co-production. Of course, all these co-production styles can be retrieved in the healthcare environment (Fotaki, 2011; Cepiku & Giordano, 2014; Van Eijk & Steen, 2016), as depicted in Fig. 2.1.

Osborne and Strokosch (2013) proposed an alternative taxonomy of co-production modes, focusing the attention on the role played by the users in the process of value co-creation. Drawing on their propositions, three co-production modes could be identified. Consumer co-production is aimed at empowering the users at the operational stage. In fact, the process of empowerment and involvement is conceived as a sheer managerial technique, which attempts to make the users aware of the attributes of the service delivery systems and to increase their compliance with the providers' instructions. The users' ability to collect value from service provision is improved, even though they only partially participate in service design and delivery (Gómez & Jaglin, 2016). Participative co-production goes beyond the operational level, since it concerns both the delivery, the design and the planning of existing services. In this case, user involvement is mainly intended to improve the quality of public services. In fact, users contribute in increasing the effectiveness and the responsiveness of public services by bringing innovative perspectives and non-conventional ideas (Tuurnas, 2015). Last but not least, enhanced co-production challenges the traditional provider-led model of public service provision. Users are understood as the driving

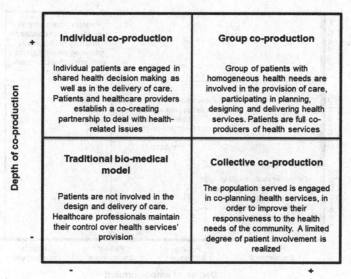

Fig. 2.1 Co-production styles in the healthcare environment. *Source* Author's elaboration

forces of transformational innovations, which bring toward new forms of user-provider relationships (Hennala & Melkas, 2016). In other words, the users perform as value co-creators both in the delivery of public services and in supporting the public sector organizations to anticipate the future needs of the community.

Also, these co-production modes could be easily retrieved in the healthcare service system. Consumer co-production is the more common co-production mode when the provision of health services is concerned. It requires a limited degree of patient empowerment. In fact, the patients are partially engaged in the healthcare delivery system, in order to increase their compliance with medical prescriptions (McGuckin, Storr, Longtin, Allegranzi, & Pittet, 2011). Alternatively, participative co-production requires a greater level of patient empowerment. In order to allow the patients to participate in the process of value co-creation, both engagement and involvement are required, beyond enablement and activation. From this point of view, participative co-production could be understood as a step forward in health services' co-production, as compared with consumer co-production. It paves the way for a wider patient involvement, producing greater satisfaction and better service quality (Gill, White, & Cameron, 2011). Enhanced co-production entails a full-fledged process of patient empowerment, who perform as the main drivers of innovation and change within the healthcare service system (BMJ, 2016). This is possible by raising the patients' awareness of their co-producing potential and encouraging them to broadly collaborate with the healthcare providers, in order to achieve better health outcomes (Morgan et al., 2016).

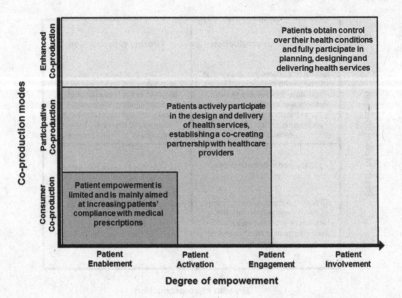

Fig. 2.2   Co-production modes and levels of patient empowerment. *Source* Author's elaboration

Figure 2.2 depicts the co-production modes suggested by Osborne and Strokosch (2013), pointing out a relationship between each of them and the levels of patient empowerment. While a limited degree of patient empowerment is consistent with consumer co-production, enhanced co-production requires an expert patient to be realized.

2.3   A Re-design of the Patient-Provider Relationship

It is interesting to point out that health services' co-production basically involves a reconfiguration of the roles of patients and healthcare providers during the medical encounter, recognizing them as partners. In an attempt to systematize the consequences of co-production on the patient-provider relationship, the theoretical framework proposed by Bovaird (2007) could be exploited. Going more into details, a diversified range of professional-user relationships could be identified, which are disentangled by taking into consideration the way regular providers and consumer producers—both individually and collectively—perform the activities of service co-planning, co-design and co-delivery. Table 2.2 illustrates the different shades of co-producing relationship between the providers and the users, in light of their specific role in a generic service delivery system.

The columns of Table 2.2 show the distribution of responsibilities between the professionals and the users with regard to the planning and/or the design of services. Alternatively, the rows depict the allocation of functions between the

Table 2.2 Co-production styles and users-providers relationship

		Service design and planning		
		Providers as sole service designers and planners	Providers and users as service co-planners and co-designers	Users as sole service designers and planners
Service delivery	Providers as sole service deliverers	*Traditional service provision*: Professionals as sole value creators in the service delivery system	*Service co-planning and co-design*: Users participate in planning and designing services, which are delivered by traditional providers	*Professional delivery of user-led services*: Users plan and design services, which are delivered by traditional providers
	Providers and users as service co-deliverers	*Service co-delivery*: Professionals as sole planner and designer of services and engagement of users as co-deliverers	*Full co-production*: Establishment of a co-creating partnership between the users and the providers	*Co-delivery of user-led services*: Users plan and design services, which are delivered in partnership by users and traditional providers
	Users as sole service deliverers	*User delivery of provider-led services*: Professionals as sole planner and designer of services and engagement of users as co-deliverers	*Co-design of user-led services*: Users participate in planning and designing services and perform as the sole deliverer of services	*Self-organized provision*: Users as sole value creators in the service delivery system

Source Author's adaptation from Bovaird (2007)

providers and the users concerning the delivery of services. Crossing the rows and the columns, 9 different approaches to service co-production could be identified.

When the planning, design and delivery of services are exclusively led by ordinary providers, a traditional approach to service provision occurs. Users are understood as mere consumers of value, which is solely created by providers. Therefore, the users are not involved in service provision, sticking to a relieving logic. In several circumstances, the users could be engaged in planning services, assuming a limited role in delivering them. In other words, the traditional service provision could be contaminated with the involvement of users in planning and designing services, in order to make the latter more compliant with the perceived needs of the population served. On the other hand, the users could be involved in delivering services, while planning activities continue to be controlled by regular providers. In this case, the users co-deliver services which are designed by professionals, with the purpose of complementing the efforts of providing organizations and improving their responsiveness.

Also, users could be engaged as the sole providers of professionally designed services, thus performing as key partners of providing institutions in the process of value creation, even though they are not assigned with a relevant role in planning the attributes of the service delivery system. Besides, users could perform as sole deliverers of co-planned services: in this specific circumstance, the users and the providers collaborate in defining the characteristics of services, whose implementation is exclusively ascribed to the former. Lastly, users could perform as co-deliverers of services which are planned without the contribution of regular providers, performing as the most important driver of value creation in the service delivery system. In all of these cases, only a shade of service co-production is caught. In fact, the users and the providers variously collaborate to plan, design and deliver the service, but they do not share the same responsibilities to contribute in the proper functioning of the service delivery system. From this point of view, full co-production is only realized when regular providers and users are simultaneously engaged in co-planning, co-designing, and co-delivering services, performing as peers in the process of value co-creation.

The taxonomy suggested by Bovaird (2007) could be adapted in the attempt to apply it to the healthcare delivery system, as depicted in Table 2.3. In fact, the patients and the healthcare professionals could variously cooperate for the purpose of health services' design and delivery, realizing the different co-production styles briefly presented above.

Traditional service provision echoes the biomedical model, which assigns to patients a limited role in co-producing health services and conceives the healthcare providers as the main value creators during the medical encounter (Lewis, 2009). Sticking to a traditional service provision, patient empowerment is neglected; in fact, the attention is focused on the disease, as well as on the relieving ability of healthcare professionals.

In several cases, patients are enabled to participate in the delivery of care, even though the healthcare professionals maintain the control over health decision making. In this circumstance, the process of empowerment is aimed at improving the ability of the patients to comply with the clinical prescriptions of healthcare professionals and to stick to the requirements of the health treatment, thus performing as active co-deliverers of care (Delamater, 2006). Also, it is possible that the healthcare professionals support and encourage the patients to be the sole deliverers of health services which are professionally planned and designed. That is to say, the patients may act as self-carers of their own health conditions, developing the skills and the competencies to cope with their health-related problems according to the prescriptions of healthcare professionals (Inouye, Flannelly, & Flannelly, 2001).

The patients could be involved as co-planners and co-designers of health services, partnering with the healthcare professionals to define and deliver an appropriate health treatments. On the one hand, the healthcare professionals could

Table 2.3 Co-production styles and patients-providers relationship in healthcare

		Health service design and planning		
		Providers as sole service designers and planners	Providers and users as service co-planners and co-designers	Users as sole service designers and planners
Health service delivery	Providers as sole service deliverers	*Traditional service provision*: Healthcare professionals stick to the biomedical model, focusing on the illness rather than on patients' health needs	*Service co-planning and co-design*: Healthcare professionals involve users in shared decision making, but maintain their control over healthcare delivery	*Professional delivery of patient-led services*: Patients are the main drivers of health decisions, while healthcare professionals perform as the sole deliverer of care
	Providers and users as service co-deliverers	*Service co-delivery*: Healthcare professionals control health decision making and involve patients in delivering health services	*Full co-production*: Establishment of a partnership between the patients and the providers to plan, design and deliver health services	*Co-delivery of patient-led services*: Patients control health decision making and partner with healthcare professionals to deliver health services
	Users as sole service deliverers	*Patient delivery of provider-led services*: Healthcare Professionals plan and design health services, which are delivered by patients through self-care	*Co-design of patient-delivered services*: Patients are involved in shared decision making and are engaged in self-managing health services	*Self-organized provision*: Patients self-organize healthcare provision and do not establish a co-creating partnership with the healthcare providers

Source Author's elaboration

perform as the sole deliverer of co-planned and co-designed services: this is possible when the patients are allowed to participate in shared decision making, concurring in planning health treatments (Frosch & Kaplan, 1999; Hargraves, LeBlanc, Shah, & Montori, 2016). On the other hand, the patients could be engaged as the main deliverers of co-planned health treatments, being encouraged to be autonomous in protecting and promoting their well-being (Kennedy et al., 2013), even though relying on the support of the healthcare professionals (Veroff, Marr, & Wennberg, 2013).

In rare cases, the patients could perform as the sole planners and designers of health services, which could be either co-delivered or delivered by healthcare professionals. In the former case, the healthcare professionals strives for promoting patients' independence (Hughes, 2003); in the latter case, the healthcare providers support the patients' self-management of care, being involved in the delivery of person-centered care (Eaton, Roberts, & Turner, 2015).

As previously emphasized, all these situations concern a particular shade of health services co-production. Indeed, full health services co-production is only realized when the patients and the healthcare professionals fully collaborate in co-planning, co-designing and co-delivering health treatments, establishing a therapeutic alliance which is aimed to the protection and the promotion of psycho-physical well-being (Palumbo, 2016; Clark, 2015). Obviously, the implementation of such a co-creating partnership requires a twofold process of empowerment, which should concern both the patients and the healthcare professionals.

2.4   The Effects of Patient Empowerment on Health Outcomes

A "*zest for patient empowerment*" has risen in the last few years (Raina & Thawani, 2016, p. 1). In fact, patient empowerment has been depicted as a crucial tool to increase the effectiveness and the sustainability of the healthcare service system (Adinolfi, Starace, & Palumbo, 2016). Patient empowerment has been attached to different categories of patients and various health conditions. Among others, scholars have stressed the role of patient empowerment in improving the access to care of disadvantaged populations (Lubetkin, Lu, & Gold, 2010). In fact, patient empowerment shrinks the barriers to patient activation and increases the patients' commitment to health protection and promotion, thus leading to a better use of health services available. Similarly, patient empowerment has been pointed out as an important strategy to deal with rare diseases (Aymé, Kole, & Groft, 2008). In this specific circumstance, the process of empowerment allows to awaken the sleeping resources of patients, who are encouraged to participate—both individually and collectively—in co-designing and co-delivering appropriate health services.

Also, patient empowerment has been claimed to be especially fitting with the treatment of long-term conditions (Greenhalgh, 2009). Actually, people who live with one or more chronic conditions may strongly benefit from patient empowerment initiatives. In particular, the engagement of chronic patients in healthcare delivery allows the access to more personalized and timely care, which in turn contributes in increasing the appropriateness of care (Fotaki, 2011). It is worth noting that the importance of patient empowerment has been claimed beyond chronic and rare conditions, representing the underpinning of patient-centeredness in the healthcare service system also when acute diseases are concerned (de Boer, Delnoij, & Rademakers, 2013).

Two different interpretations of patient empowerment have been suggested in order to examine its consequences on health outcomes. On the one hand, patient empowerment has been dealt with as a risk factor (Simmons, Wolever, Bechard, & Snyderman, 2014): it involves the development of the individual knowledge, confidence and skills to cope with the disease and to protect the individual well-being. From this point of view, the disempowerment of patients may produce several side effects on health outcomes, preventing the patients to participate in the provision of care and to perform as value co-creators during the medical encounter. On the other hand, patient empowerment has been understood as an outcome of enhanced patient-provider relationships (McAllister, Dunn, Payne, Davies, & Todd, 2012), which pave the way for a greater willingness to activate and use the patients' sleeping resources in order to enhance the functioning of the healthcare delivery system. Regardless of the interpretation embraced, a link between patient empowerment and health outcomes could be figured out (Palumbo, 2016). However, the scientific literature is not consistent in discussing the direction and the intensity of such a relationship (Michie, Miles, & Weinman, 2003).

Therefore, it is not surprising that the relation between patient empowerment and health outcomes has been argued to be complex and dynamic. In general terms, since it involves a long-term partnership between the patients and the members of the healthcare service system at both the operative and the strategic levels, patient empowerment establishes a bridge for the achievement of more responsive and effective care, which is crucial to achieve increased health outcomes (Laurance et al., 2014). Echoing these considerations, a co-creating relationship between the patients and the providers of care has been found to be related with higher rates of compliance and therapeutic adherence, resulting in better recovery and enhanced health outcomes (Skolasky, Mackenzie, Wegener, & Riley, 2011). Similarly, Hibbard and Greene (2013) pointed out a positive link between patient empowerment and better healthcare experiences, with empowered patients being more willing to participate in the provision of care and to perform as active value co-creators. Of course, the more the patients are able and willing to be involved in the provision of care, the higher their retention rates and their attendance to health services in order to cope with impaired health conditions, and, consequently, the better the health outcomes achievable (Alegría et al., 2008).

Also, empowered patients have been found to show greater use of preventive health services and to be more likely to follow healthy behaviors, which are significant predictors of better health outcomes (Greene, Hibbard, Sacks, Overton, & Parrotta, 2015). What is even more interesting is that the effects of patient empowerment on the ability of the patients to perform as value co-creators and service co-producers have been argued to be enduring, paving the way for the establishment of a long-term collaborative partnership between the patients and the healthcare providers (Hibbard, Greene, Shi, Mittler, & Scanlon, 2015). In fact, patient empowerment entails: better patient-provider communications, increased patients' satisfaction and greater compliance with medical prescriptions, which are key to produce patient engagement and to enhance health outcomes (Powers & Bendall, 2004).

Interestingly, patient empowerment has been related to a more appropriate access to care. Empowered patients living with one or more chronic conditions have been found to be less likely to use health services and to be more effective in following medical prescriptions, thus reporting better health outcomes as compared with those who were not involved in co-planning and co-delivering health services (Remmers et al., 2009). Confirming the role of patient empowerment in producing a more appropriate access to care, Mitchell et al. (2013) reported that hospitalized patients who were not involved in patient empowerment initiatives were more likely to use hospital services within 30 days after discharge. This was especially true for emergency services, emphasizing that lower health outcomes are associated with poorer levels of patient activation. In spite of these findings, scholars are not consistent in depicting a positive relationship between patient empowerment and health outcomes when hospitalized patients are concerned (Arnetz et al., 2010). In particular, the hostility of the hospital setting could be argued to prevent the effectiveness of patient empowerment initiatives, producing apprehension and disengagement.

The relationship between patient empowerment and health outcomes is mediated by different variables, which could amplify or reduce the impacts of interventions intended to enable and involve the patients in the provision of health services. First of all, patient empowerment is strictly related to the ability of the patients to access, understand and use health information (Smith, Pandit, Rush, Wolf, & Simon, 2015). Moreover, the lack of reliable and significant health information within the healthcare service system could negatively affect the ability of the patients to participate in the provision of care and to perform as value co-creators (Annarumma & Palumbo, 2016). Information and communication technologies represent a fundamental tool to enhance the access of patients to timely and reliable health information, thus performing as an essential catalyst to patient empowerment initiatives (Samoocha, Bruinvels, Elbers, Anema, & van der Beek, 2010). Beyond fostering the patients' access to health information, digital tools are able to create a social arena which encourage the establishment of co-creating relationships between the patients and the healthcare professionals, facilitating the mutual exchange of information (Bartlett & Coulson, 2011).

Both health outcomes and patients' satisfaction rely on the establishment of a trusted and friendly patient-provider relationship. At the same time, it is worth noting that patient empowerment and other similar initiatives aimed at supporting the patients' autonomy in the healthcare environment have been found to produce trust and satisfaction among the patients, which in turn contributes in improving the experience of care (Lee & Lin, 2010). On the one hand, trust is fostered by the increased control of patients over the process of health service design and delivery and, on the other hand, by the continuous support of patients' activation by the side of healthcare professionals (Ouschan, Sweeney, & Johnson, 2006).

The importance of trust and reliable patient-provider communication is particularly relevant when disadvantaged patients are concerned, since they are more likely to escape patient empowerment initiatives (Maly, Stein, Umezawa, Leake, & Anglin, 2008). From this point of view, it could be maintained that, if patient empowerment initiatives are not supported by the establishment of more direct and friendly relationships between the patients and the healthcare professionals, their effects on health outcomes turn out to be constrained (Street et al., 2009). On the opposite, the commitment of healthcare professionals to provide the patients with tailored communication tools in order to promote their involvement in health service co-production is expected to pave the way for a more appropriate use of health services and, as a consequence, for better health outcomes (Trummer, Mueller, Nowak, Stidl, & Pelikan, 2006).

Last but not least, the relationship between patient empowerment and health outcomes is mediated by the disease-specific knowledge of patients. In fact, scholars have emphasized that patient activation is associated with an increased ability of patients to develop an adequate understanding of their health condition, as well as with a higher awareness of the implications of the disease on psycho-physical well-being (Hendriks & Rademakers, 2014). Disease-related knowledge leads to greater patients' ability to self-manage their health conditions, which is related to the achievement of better health outcomes (Camerini, Schulz, & Nakamoto, 2012). Ultimately, patient empowerment initiatives assist the patients in developing both health-related skills and increased self-efficacy, which underpin self-management of care and concur in improving the individual well-being (Shah & Siegel, 2015).

Figure 2.3 summarizes the relationship which links patient empowerment and health outcomes. The scientific literature is consistent in discussing the positive effects of patient empowerment programmes on health outcomes (Altshuler et al., 2016). However, in most of the cases the variables which mediate the relationship between patient empowerment and health outcomes have been overlooked. There is a strong need for shedding light on these mediating variables, in order to push forward the knowledge about the consequences of patient empowerment initiatives.

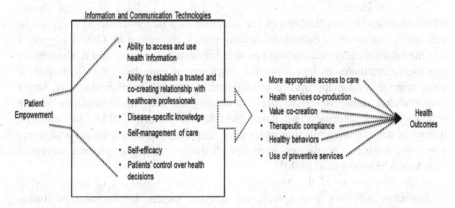

Fig. 2.3 The relationship linking patient empowerment and health outcomes. *Source* Author's elaboration

The greater awareness of the mediating variables between patient empowerment interventions and health outcomes could bring to the design of more effective and tailored patient empowerment interventions, improving the involvement of patients in the delivery of care.

Patient empowerment implies the activation of the patients' sleeping resources. Such a process of activation concerns the ability of the patients to access, understand, process and use health information, their willingness to establish a co-creating partnership with the healthcare professionals, the development of disease-specific knowledge and the proficiency in self-managing health conditions. Information and communication technologies create a digital arena which allows to strengthen the link between patient empowerment initiatives and health outcomes, disintermediating the relationship between the patients and the healthcare providers. Hence, information and communication technologies may foster the patients' ability to perform as value co-creators in the healthcare service system.

2.5   Patient Empowerment: A Requisite for Sustainability

Inadequate patient empowerment has been discussed as an important determinant of inefficient management of impaired health conditions (Angelmar & Berman, 2007). In particular, patient disempowerment is associated with inadequate ability to detect and cope with health problems, limited involvement in co-planning and co-designing health treatments, poor willingness to participate in the delivery of care, low compliance with medication prescriptions and higher risks of inappropriate access to care (Palumbo, Annarumma, Adinolfi, & Musella, 2016). From this point of view, it could be pointed out that patient disempowerment is associated with higher healthcare costs. Therefore, if patient empowerment is not included among the strategic priorities of the healthcare service system, significant risks of unsustainability are expected to emerge.

These considerations seem to be supported by the findings of several studies which examine the implications of the adoption of a patient-centered approach to care during the medical encounter. Among others, Stewart et al. (2000) suggested that the establishment of a common ground between the patients and the healthcare providers contributes in increasing the efficiency of care, by reducing diagnostic tests, referrals and inappropriate use of health services. In a similar way, lower health-related charges have been attached to the implementation of a patient-centered approach to care (Bertakis & Azari, 2011). In addition, patient-centered communication styles have been found to be associated with fewer diagnostic testing expenditures, even though they are likely to produce increased visit length (Epstein et al., 2005).

Since time is one of the most critical and scarce resources in the healthcare environment, scholars have questioned whether patient involvement is always possible when designing and delivering health services (Jones et al., 2004). In fact, it is possible that the healthcare professionals overlook the role played by patient empowerment in their everyday practices, since they lack adequate time to meet the special information and health needs of their patients. Nonetheless, it is interesting to note that the initiatives aimed at promoting patient empowerment have been generally found to be cost effective, merging two conflicting purposes: the enhancement of health outcomes and the containment of costs associated with the provision of care (Richardson et al., 2008). As anticipated, this is possible by enabling the sleeping resources of the patients and activating them for the purposes of health protection and promotion.

Empowered patients perceive greater self-efficacy in dealing with their health-related conditions and are likely to report a lower use of emergency and hospital services (Shively et al., 2013), thus contributing to significant cost savings (Lorig et al., 2001). Hence, it is not surprising that a recent study aimed at investigating the costs incurred by patients facing different diseases—such as diabetes, hyperlipidemia, hypertension and asthma—reported that those living with higher levels of patient activation were consistent in producing lower healthcare costs as compared with their disempowered counterparts (Hibbard, Greene, & Overton, 2013). A more appropriate access to care and healthier life-styles have been argued to perform as the most important determinants of reduced costs for empowered patients (Greene & Hibbard, 2012). Also, patient empowerment has been claimed to enhance the ability and the willingness of patients to take a proactive role in the healthcare service system, partnering the providers of care in co-producing health services and co-creating value (Tzeng et al., 2015).

Since it merges the opportunity to reduce health costs and to increase health outcomes (Goozner, 2016), patient empowerment could be depicted as a requisite for increased sustainability of the healthcare service system (Angelmar & Berman, 2007). A wide-ranging analysis should be performed to appreciate the impact of patient empowerment initiatives on the functioning of the healthcare system, taking into considerations both the cost savings associated with the engagement of patients in the provision of care and the additional costs which are required to enable patients (Entwistle, Sowden, & Watt, 1998). Embracing such perspective, Groessl and Cronan (2000) claimed that the cost savings which are associated with patient empowerment are able to outweigh the costs of planning and implementing patient empowerment initiatives. Drawing on these arguments, greater attention should be paid to the role of patient empowerment in strengthening the sustainability of the healthcare service system, a hot topic in most of Western Countries' health reform.

References

Adinolfi, P., Starace, F., & Palumbo, R. (2016). Health outcomes and patient empowerment. The case of health budgets in Italy. *Journal of Health Management, 18*(1), 117–133.
Alegría, M., Polo, A., Gao, S., Santana, L., Rothstein, D., Jimenez, A., et al. (2008). Evaluation of a patient activation and empowerment intervention in mental health care. *Medical Care, 46*(3), 247–256.

Altshuler, L., Plaksin, J., Zabar, S., Wallach, A., Sawicki, C., Kundrod, S., & Kalet, A. (2016). Transforming the Patient Role to Achieve Better Outcomes Through a Patient Empowerment Program: A Randomized Wait-List Control Trial Protocol. *JMIR research protocols, 5*(2), e68

Angelmar, R., & Berman, P. C. (2007). *Patient empowerment and efficient health outcomes.* Luxembourg: Luxembourg's Ministry of Health, Sitra and Pfizer Inc.

Annarumma, C., & Palumbo, R. (2016). Contextualizing health literacy to health care organizations: Exploratory insights. *Journal of Health Management, 18*(4), 611–624.

Arnetz, J. E., Winblad, U., Hoglund, A. T., Lindahl, B., Spangberg, K., Wallentin, L., et al. (2010). Is patient involvement during hospitalization for acute myocardial infarction associated with post-discharge treatment outcome? An exploratory study. *Health Expectations*, 298–311.

Aymé, S., Kole, A., & Groft, S. (2008). Empowerment of patients: Lessons from the rare diseases community. *Lancet, 371*(9629), 2048–2051.

Bartlett, Y. K., & Coulson, N. S. (2011). An investigation into the empowerment effects of using online support groups and how this affects health professional/patient communication. *Patient Education and Counseling, 83*(1), 113–119.

Bertakis, K. D., & Azari, R. (2011). Determinants and outcomes of patient-centered care. *Patient Education and Counseling, 85*(1), 46–52.

Bettencourt, L. A., Ostrom, A. L., Brown, S. W., & Roundtree, R. I. (2002). Client co-production in knowledge-intensive business services. *California Management Review, 44,* 100–128.

BMJ. (2016). Co-creating health: more than a dream. *British Medical Journal, 354*(i4550). doi:10. 1136/bmj.i4550

Bovaird, T. (2007). Beyond engagement and participation: User and community co-production of public services. *Public Administration Review, 67*(5), 846–860.

Bovaird, T., Van Ryzin, G. G., Loeffler, E., & Parrado, S. (2015). Activating citizens to participate in collective co-production of public services. *Journal of Social Policy, 44*(1), 1–23.

Brudney, J. L., & England, R. E. (1983). Toward a definition of the coproduction concept. *Public Administration Review, 43*(1), 59–65.

Camerini, L., Schulz, P. J., & Nakamoto, K. (2012). Differential effects of health knowledge and health empowerment over patients' self-management and health outcomes: A cross-sectional evaluation. *Patient Education and Counseling, 89*(2), 337–344.

Cegala, D. J., Street, R. L., Jr., & Clinch, R. (2007). The impact of patient participation on physicians' information provision during a primary care medical interview. *Health Communication, 21*(2), 177–185.

Cepiku, D., & Giordano, F. (2014). Co-Production in developing countries: Insights from the community health workers experience. *Public Management Review, 16*(3), 317–340.

Clark, M. (2015). Co-production in mental health care. *Mental Health Review Journal, 20*(4), 213–219.

Cramm, J. M., & Nieboer, A. P. (2015). The importance of productive patient–professional interaction for the well-being of chronically ill patients. *Quality of Life Research, 24*(4), 897–903.

Dahlberg, K. (1996). Intersubjective meeting in holistic caring: A Swedish perspective. *Nursing Science Quarterly, 9,* 147–151.

Davis, R. E., Jacklin, R., Sevdalis, N., & Vincent, C. A. (2007). Patient involvement in patient safety: What factors influence patient participation and engagement? *Health Expectations, 10* (3), 259–267.

de Boer, D., Delnoij, D., & Rademakers, J. (2013). The importance of patient-centered care for various patient groups. *Patient Education and Counseling, 90*(3), 405–410.

Delamater, A. M. (2006). Improving patient adherence. *Clinical Diabetes, 24*(2), 71–77.

Eaton, S., Roberts, S., & Turner, B. (2015). Delivering person centred care in long term conditions. *British Medical Journal.* doi:10.1136/bmj.h181

Elg, M., Engström, J., Witell, L., & Poksinska, B. (2012). Co-creation and learning in health-care service development. *Journal of Service Management, 23*(3), 328–343.

Entwistle, V. A., Sowden, A. J., & Watt, I. S. (1998). Evaluating interventions to promote patient involvement in decision-making: By what criteria should effectiveness be judged? *Journal of Health Services Research and Policy, 3*(2), 100–107.

Epstein, R. M., Franks, P., Shields, C., Meldrum, S. C., Miller, K. N., Campbell, T. L., et al. (2005). Patient-centered communication and diagnosis testing. *Annals of Family Medicine, 3* (5), 415–421.

Fotaki, M. (2011). Towards developing new partnerships in public services: Users as consumers, citizens and/or co-producers in health and social care in England and Sweden. *Public Administration, 89*(3), 933–955.

Freidson, E. (1970). *Professional dominance: The social structure of medical care.* New York: Atherton Press.

Freire, P. (1993). *Pedagogy of the oppressed.* New York: Continuum.

Frosch, D. L., & Kaplan, R. M. (1999). Shared decision making in clinical medicine: Past research and future directions. *American Journal of Preventive Medicine, 17*(4), 285–294.

Gill, L., White, L., & Cameron, I. D. (2011). Service co-creation in community-based aged healthcare. *Managing Service Quality: An International Journal, 21*(2), 152–177.

Gómez, C. D., & Jaglin, S. (2016). When urban modernisation entails service delivery co-production: a glance from Medellin. *Urban Research & Practice.* Published on-line ahead of print on March 11, 2016. doi:10.1080/17535069.2016.1156734

Goozner, M. (2016). Patient empowerment through shared decisions can lower costs. *Modern Healthcare, 46*(4), 24.

Greene, J., & Hibbard, J. H. (2012). Why does patient activation matter? An examination of the relationships between patient activation and health-related outcomes. *Journal of General Internal Medicine, 27*(5), 520–526.

Greene, J., Hibbard, J. H., Sacks, R., Overton, V., & Parrotta, C. D. (2015). When patient activation levels change, health outcomes and costs change, too. *Health Affairs, 34*(3), 431–437.

Greenhalgh, T. (2009). Patient and public involvement in chronic illness: Beyond the expert patient. *British Medical Journal, 338*(b49). doi:10.1136/bmj.b49

Groessl, E. J., & Cronan, T. A. (2000). A cost analysis of self-management programs for people with chronic illness. *American Journal of Community Psychology, 28*(4), 455–480.

Guadagnoli, E., & Ward, P. (1998). Patient participation in decision making. *Social Science and Medicine, 47*(3), 329–339.

Hardyman, W., Daunt, K. L., & Kitchener, M. (2015). Value co-creation through patient engagement in health care: A micro-level approach and research agenda. *Public Management Review, 17*(1), 90–107.

Hargraves, I., LeBlanc, A., Shah, N. D., & Montori, V. M. (2016). Shared decision making: The need for patient-clinician conversation, not just information. *Health Affairs, 35*(4), 627–629.

Hendriks, M., & Rademakers, J. (2014). Relationships between patient activation, disease-specific knowledge and health outcomes among people with diabetes; a survey study. *BMC Health Services Research, 14*(393). doi:10.1186/1472-6963-14-393

Hennala, L., & Melkas, H. (2016). Understanding users' collective voice in public service innovation. *Knowledge and Process Management, 23*(1), 62–72.

Hibbard, J. H., & Greene, J. (2013). What the evidence shows about patient activation: Better health outcomes and care experiences; fewer data on costs. *Health Affairs, 32*(2), 207–214.

Hibbard, J. H., Greene, J., & Overton, V. (2013). Patients with lower activation associated with higher costs; delivery systems should know their patients' 'scores'. *Health Affairs, 32*(2), 216–222.

Hibbard, J. H., Greene, J., Shi, Y., Mittler, J., & Scanlon, D. (2015). Taking the long view: How well do patient activation scores predict outcomes four years later? *Medical Care Research and Review, 72*(3), 324–337.

Hughes, S. (2003). Promoting independence: The nurse as coach. *Nursing Standard, 18*(4), 42–44.

Inouye, J., Flannelly, L., & Flannelly, K. J. (2001). The effectiveness of self-management training for individuals with HIV/AIDS. *Journal of the Association of Nurses in AIDS Care, 12*(5), 71–82.

Jones, I. R., Berney, L., Kelly, M., Doyal, L., Griffiths, C., Feder, G., et al. (2004). Is patient involvement possible when decisions involve scarce resources? A qualitative study of decision-making in primary care. *Social Science and Medicine, 59*(1), 93–102.

Kennedy, A., Bower, P., Reeves, D., Blakeman, T., Bowen, R., Chew-Graham, C., et al. (2013). Implementation of self-management support for long term conditions in routine primary care settings: Cluster randomised controlled trial. *British Medical Journal, 246*(2882). doi:10.1136/bmj.f2882

Laurance, J., Henderson, S., Howitt, P. J., Matar, M., Al Kuwari, H., Edgman-Levitan, S., et al. (2014). Patient engagement: Four case studies that highlight the potential for improved health outcomes and reduced costs. *Health Affairs, 33*(9), 1627–1634.

Lee, Y.-Y., & Lin, J. L. (2010). Do patient autonomy preferences matter? Linking patient-centered care to patient-physician relationships and health outcomes. *Social Science and Medicine, 71* (10), 1811–1818.

Lewis, S. (2009). Seeking a new biomedical model. How evolutionary biology may contribute. *Journal of Evaluation in Clinical Practice, 15*(4), 745–748.

Loeffler, E., Power, G., Bovaird, T., & Hine-Hughes, F. (2012). *Co-production in health and social care. What it is and how to do it.* Birmingham: Governance International.

Lorig, K. R., Ritter, P., Stewart, A. L., Sobel, D. S., Brown, B. W., Bandura, A., et al. (2001). Chronic disease self-management program: 2-year health status and health care utilization outcomes. *Medical Care, 39*(11), 1217–1223.

Lubetkin, E. I., Lu, W.-H., & Gold, M. R. (2010). Levels and correlates of patient activation in health center settings: Building strategies for improving health outcomes. *Journal of Health Care for the Poor and Underserved, 21*(3), 796–808.

Maly, R. C., Stein, J. A., Umezawa, Y., Leake, B., & Anglin, M. D. (2008). Racial/ethnic differences in breast cancer outcomes among older patients: Effects of physician communication and patient empowerment. *Health Psychology, 27*(6), 728–736.

Mattingly, T. J., II., Tom, S. E., Stuart, B., & Onukwugha, E. (2016). Examining patient–provider relationship (PPR) quality and patient activation in the Medicare population. *Aging Clinical and Experimental Research*. Published on-line ahead of print on June 20, 2016. doi:10.1007/s40520-016-0600-z

McAllister, M., Dunn, G., Payne, K., Davies, L., & Todd, C. (2012). Patient empowerment: The need to consider it as a measurable patient-reported outcome for chronic conditions. *BMC Health Services Research, 12*(157). doi:10.1186/1472-6963-12-157

McColl-Kennedy, J. R., Vargo, S. L., Dagger, T. S., Sweeney, J. C., & van Kasteren, Y. (2012). Health care customer value cocreation practice styles. *Journal of Service Research, 15*(4), 370–389.

McGuckin, M., Storr, J., Longtin, Y., Allegranzi, B., & Pittet, D. (2011). Patient empowerment and multimodal hand hygiene promotion: A win-win strategy. *American Journal of Medical Quality, 26*(1), 10–17.

McLaughlin, H. (2004). Partnerships: Panacea or pretence? *Journal of Interprofessional Care, 18* (2), 103–113.

Mead, N., & Bower, P. (2000). Patient-centredness: A conceptual framework and review of the empirical literature. *Social Science and Medicine, 51,* 1087–1110.

Michie, S., Miles, J., & Weinman, J. (2003). Patient-centredness in chronic illness: What is it and does it matter? *Patient Education and Counseling, 51*(3), 197–206.

Mitchell, S. E., Gardiner, P. M., Sadikova, E., Martin, J. M., Jack, B. W., Hibbard, J. H., et al. (2013). Patient activation and 30-day post-discharge hospital utilization. *Journal of General Internal Medicine, 29*(2), 349–355.

Moll, J. (2010). The patient as service co-creator. In *Proceedings of the 11th Biennial Participatory Design Conference* (pp. 163–166). November 29–December 3, 2010. Sydney.

Morgan, H. M., Entwistle, V. A., Cribb, A., Christmas, S., Owens, J., Skea, Z. C., et al. (2016). We need to talk about purpose: A critical interpretive synthesis of health and social care professionals' approaches to self-management support for people with long-term conditions. *Health Expectations*. Published on-line ahead of print on April 14, 2016. doi:10.1111/hex. 12453

Murray, B., & McCrone, S. (2015). An integrative review of promoting trust in the patient–primary care provider relationship. *Journal of Advanced Nursing, 71*(1), 3–23.

Needham, C. (2012). *Co-production: An emerging evidence base for adult social care transformation*. London: Social Care Institute for Excellence.

Osborne, S. P., & Strokosch, K. (2013). It takes two to tango? Understanding the co-production of public services by integrating the services management and public administration perspectives. *British Journal of Management, 24*(S1), 31–47.

Ostrom, V., & Ostrom, E. (1977). Public goods and public choices. In E. Savas (Ed.), *Alternatives for delivering public services. Toward improved performance* (pp. 7–49). Boulder, CO: Westview.

Ouschan, R., Sweeney, J., & Johnson, L. (2006). Customer empowerment and relationship outcomes in healthcare consultations. *European Journal of Marketing, 40*(9–10), 1068–1086.

Palumbo, R. (2015). The dark side of health care co-production. Health literacy as a requisite for the co-production of care. *International Journal of Social Science & Human Behavior Study, 2* (1), 82–86.

Palumbo, R. (2016). Contextualizing co-production of health care: A systematic literature review. *International Journal of Public Sector Management, 29*(1), 72–90.

Palumbo, R., Annarumma, C., Adinolfi, P., & Musella, M. (2016). The missing link to patient engagement in Italy. The role of health literacy in enabling patients. *Journal of Health Organization and Management, 30*(8), 1183–1203.

Parks, R. B., Baker, P. C., Kiser, L., Oakerson, R., Ostrom, E., Ostrom, V., et al. (1981). Consumers as coproducers of public services: Some economic and institutional considerations. *Policy Studies Journal, 9*(7), 1001–1011.

Pawlikowska, T., Zhang, W., Griffiths, F., van Dalen, J., & van der Vleuten, C. (2012). Verbal and non-verbal behavior of doctors and patients in primary care consultations—How this relates to patient enablement. *Patient Education and Counseling, 86*(1), 70–76.

Pinho, N., Beirão, G., Patrício, L., & Fisk, R. P. (2014). Understanding value co-creation in complex services with many actors. *Journal of Service Management, 25*(4), 470–493.

Pomey, M.-P., Ghadiri, D. P., Karazivan, P., Fernandez, N., & Clavel, N. (2015). Patients as partners: A qualitative study of patients' engagement in their health care. *PLoS ONE, 10*(4), e0122499.

Porter, M. E. (2010). What is value in health care? *New England Journal of Medicine, 363*(26), 2477–2481.

Powers, T. L., & Bendall, D. (2004). Improving health outcomes through patient empowerment. *Journal of Hospital Marketing & Public Relations, 15*(1), 45–59.

Prahalad, C., & Ramaswamy, V. (2004). Co-creating unique value with customers. *Strategy & Leadership, 32*(3), 4–9.

Pritchard, P., & Hughes, J. (1995). *Shared care: The future imperative?*. London: The Royal Society of Medicine Press.

Raina, R. S., & Thawani, V. (2016). The zest for patient empowerment. *Journal of Clinical and Diagnostic Research, 10*(6), 1–3.

Rathert, C., Wyrwich, M. D., & Boren, S. A. (2013). Patient-centered care and outcomes. A systematic review of the literature. *Medical Care Research and Review, 70*(4), 351–379.

Remmers, C., Hibbard, J., Mosen, D. M., Wagenfield, M., Hoye, R. E., & Jones, C. (2009). Is patient activation associated with future health outcomes and healthcare utilization among patients with diabetes? *Journal of Ambulatory Care Management, 32*(4), 320–327.

Renedo, A., Marston, C. A., Spyridonidis, D., & Barlow, J. (2015). Patient and public involvement in healthcare quality improvement: How organizations can help patients and professionals to collaborate. *Public Management Review, 17*(1), 17–34.

Richardson, G., Kennedy, A., Reeves, D., Bower, P., Lee, V., Middleton, E., et al. (2008). Cost effectiveness of the Expert Patients Programme (EPP) for patients with chronic conditions. *Journal of Epidemiology and Community Health, 62*(4), 361–367.

Riessman, F., & Banks, E. (2001). A marriage of opposites: Self-help and the health care system. *American Psychologist, 56*(2), 173–174.

Rollow, W., & Cucchiara, P. (2016). Achieving value in primary care: The primary care value model. *Annals of Family Medicine, 14*(2), 159–165.

Saha, S., Beach, M. C., & Cooper, L. A. (2008). Patient centeredness, cultural competence and healthcare quality. *Journal of National Medical Association, 100*(11), 1275–1285.

Samoocha, D., Bruinvels, D. J., Elbers, N. A., Anema, J. R., & van der Beek, A. J. (2010). Effectiveness of web-based interventions on patient empowerment: A systematic review and meta-analysis. *Journal of Medical Internet Research, 12*(2), e23.

Shah, S. L., & Siegel, C. A. (2015). Increasing patient activation could improve outcomes for patients with inflammatory bowel disease. *Inflammatory Bowel Diseases, 21*(12), 2975–2978.

Sharp, E. B. (1980). Towards a new understanding of urban services and citizen participation: The co-production concept. *Midwest Review of Public Administration, 14,* 105–118.

Shively, M. J., Gardetto, N. J., Kodiath, M. F., Kelly, A., Smith, T. L., Stepnowsky, C., et al. (2013). Effect of patient activation on self-management in patients with heart failure. *Journal of Cardiovascular Nursing, 28*(1), 20–34.

Simmons, L. A., Wolever, R. Q., Bechard, E. M., & Snyderman, R. (2014). Patient engagement as a risk factor in personalized health care: A systematic review of the literature on chronic disease. *Genome Medicine, 6*(2), 16–28.

Skolasky, R. L., Mackenzie, E. J., Wegener, S. T., & Riley, L. H., III. (2011). Patient activation and functional recovery in persons undergoing spine surgery. *Journal of Bone and Joint Surgery, 93*(18), 1665–1671.

Smith, S. G., Pandit, A., Rush, S. R., Wolf, M. S., & Simon, C. (2015). The association between patient activation and accessing online health information: Results from a national survey of US adults. *Health Expectations, 18*(6), 3262–3267.

Stewart, M., Brown, J. B., Donner, A., McWhinney, I. R., Oates, J., Weston, W. W., et al. (2000). The impact of patient-centered care on outcomes. *Journal of Family Practice, 49*(9), 796–804.

Street, R. L., Jr., Makoul, G., Arora, N. K., & Epstein, R. M. (2009). How does communication heal? Pathways linking clinician–patient communication to health outcomes. *Patient Education and Counseling, 74,* 295–301.

Takman, C. A., & Severinsson, E. I. (1999). A description of health care professionals' experiences of encounters with patients in clinical settings. *Journal of Advanced Journal, 30* (6), 1368–1374.

Tang, T. S., Funnell, M. M., Brown, M. B., & Kurlander, J. E. (2010). Self-management support in "real-world" settings: An empowerment-based intervention. *Patient Education and Counseling, 79*(2), 178–184.

Trummer, U. F., Mueller, U. O., Nowak, P., Stidl, T., & Pelikan, J. M. (2006). Does physician–patient communication that aims at empowering patients improve clinical outcome? A case study. *Patient Education and Counseling, 61*(2), 299–306.

Tu, X. (2016). Conditions for the co-production of new immigrant services in Hong Kong. *International Journal of Public Administration, 39*(13), 1067–1076.

Tuurnas, S. (2015). Learning to co-produce? The perspective of public service professionals. *International Journal of Public Sector Management, 28*(7), 583–598.

Tzeng, A., Tzeng, T. H., Vasdev, S., Grindy, A., Saleh, J. K., & Saleh, K. J. (2015). The role of patient activation in achieving better outcomes and cost-effectiveness in patient care. *Journal of Bone and Joint Surgery Reviews, 3*(1), e4.

Van Eijk, C., & Steen, T. (2016). Why engage in co-production of public services? Mixing theory and empirical evidence. *International Review of Administrative Sciences, 82*(1), 28–46.

Vargo, S. L., & Lusch, R. F. (2008). Service-dominant logic: Continuing the evolution. *Journal of the Academy of Marketing Science, 36*(1), 1–10.

Veroff, D., Marr, A., & Wennberg, D. E. (2013). Enhanced support for shared decision making reduced costs of care for patients with preference-sensitive conditions. *Health Affairs, 32*(2), 285–293.

Weaver, B. (2011). Co-Producing community justice: The transformative potential of personalisation for penal sanctions. *British Journal of Social Work, 41*(6), 1038–1057.

Weingart, S., Zhu, J., Chiappetta, L., Stuver, S. O., Schneider, E. C., Epstein, A. M., et al. (2011). Hospitalized patients' participation and its impact on quality of care and patient safety. *International Journal for Quality in Health Care, 23*(3), 269–277.

Whitaker, G. P. (1980). Coproduction: Citizen participation in service delivery. *Public Administration Review, 40*(3), 240–246.

Wirth, W. (1991). Responding to citizens' needs: From bureaucratic accountability to individual coproduction in the public sector. In F.-X. Kaufmann (Ed.), *The public sector: Challenge for coordination and learning* (pp. 69–86). Berlin: Walter de Gruyter & Co.

Yong, P. L., Olsen, L. A., & McGinnis, J. M. (2010). *Value in health care. Accounting for cost, quality, safety, outcomes, and innovation.* Washington, D.C.: National Academies Press.

Chapter 3
The Dark Side of Patient Empowerment

3.1 Is Patient Empowerment Enough?

A large part of the scientific literature discloses a positive understanding of patient empowerment (Bridges, Loukanova, & Carrera, 2009). Nonetheless, to the author's knowledge, there is little evidence on the benefits which could be ascribed to the implementation of patient empowerment initiatives (Camacho, Landman, & Stremersch, 2010; Prigge, Dietz, Homburg, Hoyer, & Burton, 2015). In addition, it is still not clear whether patient empowerment could be factually considered as a new paradigm which is inspiring the design and delivery of care through a deep redesign of the roles and relationships between the healthcare professionals and the patients (Anderson & Funnell, 2005), or it is an apparent innovation in the healthcare service system, which turns out to be unable to challenge the traditional biomedical approach to care (Salmon & Hall, 2004).

Several arguments have been raised against patient empowerment, in an attempt to shed light on the barriers to its effective accomplishment (McAllister, Dunn, Payne, Davies, & Todd, 2012). As reported by Bee, Price, Baker, and Lovell, (2015), patient engagement in co-planning and co-producing health services could be hindered by different hurdles at the individual and the organizational levels. On the one hand, the exchange relationship between the patients and the healthcare professionals may be biased, thus preventing the process of patient enablement and involvement. On the other hand, institutional and structural barriers could be found within the healthcare environment, which contribute in disengaging the patients. Obviously, it is possible that these two kinds of obstacles simultaneously affect the participation of patients in the process of value co-creation, paving the way for the failure of patient empowerment initiatives.

The original version of this chapter was revised: Figure 3.2 has been updated. The correction to this chapter is available at https://doi.org/10.1007/978-3-319-58344-0_5

© The Author(s) 2017, corrected publication 2023
P. Rocco, *The Bright Side and the Dark Side of Patient Empowerment*,
SpringerBriefs in Public Health, DOI 10.1007/978-3-319-58344-0_3

Focusing the attention on the patient-provider relationship, it has been argued that the healthcare professionals may be interested in patient empowerment interventions for selfish purposes, rather than in an attempt to enable and engage the patient in the co-production of health services. Among others, Salmon and Hall (2003) pointed out that the healthcare providers may be urged to promote patient empowerment by the desire to transfer the responsibilities for critical health decision making to the patients, who achieve control over this process (Fraenkel & McGraw, 2007) and are involved in designing a tailored health treatment (Ryan & Sysko, 2007). Moreover, it has been argued that the administrative duties which are usually associated with patient empowerment initiatives and are charged to healthcare providers may transform them in ritualized practices, which are not effective in rebalancing the distribution of power between the patients and the healthcare professionals (Patton, 2013).

What is even more interesting, is that patients are not necessarily interested in becoming involved in patient empowerment initiatives (Palumbo, 2015a). Rather, it is possible that the patients may be unwilling to obtain greater control over the process of health services' planning and design (McAllister et al. 2012). Going more into details, inadequate health-related competencies (Covolo, Rubinelli, Orizio, & Gelatti, 2012; Palumbo, Annarumma, Musella, Adinolfi, & Piscopo, 2016a) and lack of confidence by the side of patients have been claimed to perform as two relevant barriers to patient empowerment (Aujoulat, d'Hoore, & Deccache, 2007; Rogers & Dunne, 2013). This is especially true for those who suffer from acute conditions (Bion & Heffner, 2004), who may prefer to be not empowered during the medical encounter, in order to allow the healthcare providers to solely focus their attention on the clinical treatment of the illness. Echoing these arguments, Haidet, Kroll and Sharf (2006) discussed the complexity of patient involvement in health services' delivery, pointing out that the specific social context in which the patient-provider relationship takes place may hinder patient participation in value co-creation.

It is worth noting that the individual barriers to patient empowerment concur in restraining the ability of both the healthcare professionals and the patients to establish a co-creating partnership which is intended to facilitate the co-planning, co-designing and co-delivering of health services. In particular, it has been argued that three ingredients are simultaneously needed in the recipe for patient empowerment: physician support, patient control, and patient participation (Ouschan, Sweeney, & Johnson, 2003). The lack of one of these ingredients may curb the effectiveness of patient empowerment initiatives. Actually, if the healthcare professionals are not prone to assist the patients and to help them in obtaining control over health-related issues, a traditional provider-led approach to care arises, which is rooted in biomedicine and neglect the patients' health needs (Wilson, Kendall, & Brooks, 2007). Alternatively, whether the patients are either unwilling to participate in patient empowerment initiatives or unable to deal with health-related issues, the process of patients' enablement and engagement in the delivery of care is prevented, encouraging the healthcare providers to reiterate a biomedical model of care and to perform as the sole value creators (Gibson, 1991).

Eventually, the establishment of a biased patient-provider relationship could enact a disempowering dynamic, which is rooted in medical dominance (Coburn, 2006). In particular, it paves the way for: the providers' unawareness of the specific health needs of patients; the poor willingness of the healthcare professionals to engage the patients in the provision of care; and the limited participation of patients in health-related decision making (Faulkner, 2001). Such a process of patient disempowerment is especially threatening for those who show a negative mindset toward the provision of care and do not desire to be engaged in value co-creation (McWilliam, Brown, Carmichael, & Lehman, 1994). In fact, when these circumstances prevails, the patients are unable to express their autonomy during the medical encounter, being reliant on the healing activities of the healthcare professionals, who maintain their complete control over health design and delivery.

In most of the cases, the specific characteristics of the healthcare environment magnify the difficulties met by the patients and the healthcare providers to build a co-creating partnership. Dealing with this issue, scholars have argued that the healthcare settings are usually complex and difficult to navigate (Brach, Dreyer, & Schillinger, 2014), to the point that they could discourage both the healthcare providers and the patients to cooperate in value co-creation processes (Koh, Baur, Brach, Harris, & Rowden, 2013; Annarumma & Palumbo, 2016). Complex healthcare environments are expected to produce confusion by the side of patients, as well as to sterilize the efforts of the healthcare professionals which are intended to engage the patients in the delivery of care and to promote their active participation in health services' co-production.

In addition to these considerations, it is worth noting that the scientific literature is paying a growing attention to the role of healthcare organizations in facilitating the establishment of a co-creating relationship between the patients and the providers of care (Weaver, Wray, Zellin, Gautam, & Jupka, 2012). Among others, the ability of healthcare organizations to foster the access of patients to clear and reliable information, the friendliness and comfortability of the healthcare environment and the sensitivity of healthcare organizations to the special information needs of patients living with inadequate health-related knowledge have been identified as important catalysts of patient empowerment initiatives (O'Neal, Crosby, Miller, Murray, & Condren, 2013; Alper, 2015; Palumbo, 2016a).

The patients' ability to access timely and relevant information in the healthcare environment is crucial to increase their willingness to participate in the design and delivery of care and to improve the awareness of their co-production potential (Santana et al., 2011). Besides, a friendly and comfortable healthcare environment incites the patients to perform as value co-creators and to partner with the healthcare professionals in order to contribute in health protection and promotion (French & Hernandez, 2013). Last but not least, the healthcare organizations' sensitivity to the special information needs of the patients allows the healthcare providers to identify those who are at special risk of disempowerment in the healthcare service system and to devise tailored interventions which are aimed at inciting their active involvement in the provision of care (Tritter & McCallum, 2006; Adinolfi, Starace, & Palumbo, 2016).

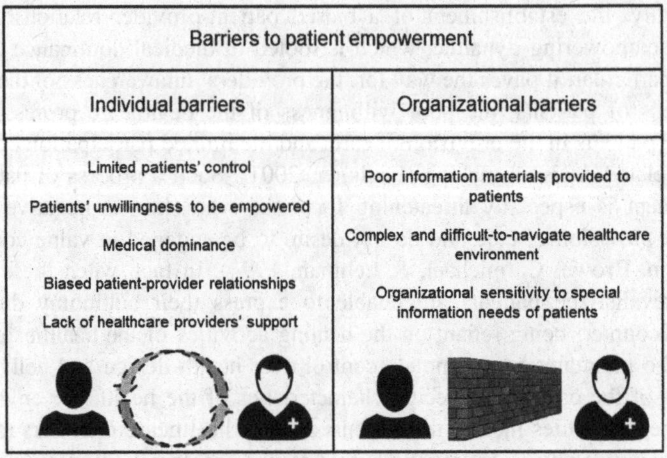

Fig. 3.1 The barriers to patient empowerment initiatives. *Source* Author's elaboration

Summarizing these points, patient empowerment initiatives may be frustrated by different barriers at both the individual and the organizational levels. Figure 3.1 helps in making this point. The effectiveness of patient empowerment depends on the ability of healthcare professionals and patients to build a trusted and reliable relationship, which allows them to perform as value co-creators rather than to stick to the traditional relieving approach, which is rooted in biomedicine. To foster the transition from biomedicine to patient-centered care, healthcare environments should be reconfigured, in an attempt to reduce their complexity and to assist the patients in navigating the healthcare service system. If individual and organizational hurdles to patient empowerment initiatives are not taken into adequate consideration, a significant risk of value co-destruction arises. In fact, rather than establishing a co-creating partnership which is intended to enable the patients' sleeping resources and activate them for the purpose of health promotion and protection, a conflictual relationship is set, which undermines the effectiveness of healthcare provision and triggers a vicious cycle of patient disengagement.

3.2 The Risks of Value Co-destruction in Service Systems

Patient empowerment is consistent with the adoption of a Service-Dominant (SD) logic perspective in the healthcare environment (Sweeney, 2007). In fact, the application of SD logic in healthcare is based on the assumption that the patients and the healthcare professionals basically interact to co-create value (Callaway & Dobrzykowski, 2009). In turn, value co-creation stems from the deep involvement of both the patients and the healthcare professionals in co-planning, co-designing and co-delivering health services (Gill, White, & Cameron, 2011).

From this point of view, it is not surprising that the antecedents of value co-creation in the healthcare environment echo what has been discussed above about the requisites to achieve patient empowerment (Merz, Czerwinski, & Merz, 2013). In particular, the patients' ability and the healthcare professionals' willingness to perform as health services' co-producers during the medical encounter have been claimed to be key issues that should be taken into account to identify and handle the opportunities of value co-creation in the healthcare environment (Edvardsson, Tronvoll, & Gruber, 2011; Lindberg, Sivberg, Willman, & Fagerström, 2015). In other words, value co-creation requires that the patients and the healthcare professionals agree to establish a trusted and long-term partnership, which is ultimately intended to activate and exploit the patients' sleeping resources for the purposes of health protection and promotion (Palumbo, 2016b).

In light of these considerations, it is possible that the patients' impaired ability to be engaged in the delivery of care and the inadequate capacity of the healthcare professionals to involve the patients in self-managing health-related issues may negatively affect the process of value co-creation. In addition, either the limited willingness of the patients to participate in the design and delivery of care or the desire of the healthcare professionals to preserve their control over health-related decisions may prevent the effectiveness of patient empowerment initiatives, paving the way for value co-destruction rather than for value co-creation (Hardyman, Daunt, & Kitchener, 2015).

Scholars from various disciplines have discussed the risks of value co-destruction in service delivery systems (Echeverri & Skålén, 2011), in an attempt to challenge the positive interpretation that has been traditionally attached to user engagement (Prahalad & Ramaswamy, 2004). Drawing on their insights, it is crucial to shed light on the potential determinants of co-destroying relationships between the users and the providers, in order to inspire the arrangement of effective coping strategies aimed at encouraging value co-creation.

Embracing a role theory perspective, Sjödin, Parida and Wincent (2016) emphasized the importance of role ambiguity in producing increased risks of value co-destruction in service delivery systems. In fact, the shift toward user engagement is necessarily associated with a change of role expectations and role descriptions by the side of both the users and the providers (Chan, Yim, & Lam, 2010). As a consequence, if the users and the providers do not have adequate information, knowledge and skills to deal with such transformation of roles, cooperative relationships are undermined by greater uncertainty and interpersonal stress, which may trigger value co-destruction dynamics (Örtqvist & Wincent, 2006).

On the one hand, the users may be not aware of what they are required to do in order to perform their role of value co-creators in the healthcare environment; moreover, they could be unwilling to partner with the providers in order to participate in service co-production (Vargo, Maglio, & Akaka, 2008). On the other hand, the providers themselves may be discouraged from engaging the users, due to worries about opportunism and uncertainty; as well, the rise of higher complexity in managing their relationship with the users could restrain the providers from arranging and implementing user engagement interventions (Grönroos & Ravald, 2011; Ciasullo, Palumbo, & Troisi, 2017).

Sticking to these propositions, Plé and Cáceres (2010) pointed out that interactional processes of value co-destruction may emerge from enhanced relationships between the users and the providers. Value co-destruction is mainly produced by a misuse of available resource by either the users, the providers, or both of them. Different causes have been argued to pave the way for such interactional processes of value co-destruction. Going more into details, the propensity of the providers and the users to participate in co-planning, co-designing and co-delivering services by embracing conflicting perspectives, bringing incongruent inputs and aiming at diverging ends has been depicted as an important determinant of co-destroying relationships (Smith, 2013). It is worth noting that the process of interactional value co-destruction may be either accidental, in the hypothesis that the providers and the users are unaware of the potential clashes between the inputs they bring in co-production activities, or intentional, in the hypothesis that they purposely strive for protecting egoistic interests during the process of service provision (Plé & Cáceres, 2010). In both the cases, a deterioration of value occurs, which is able to deeply affect the users and providers' well-being (Kuppelwieser & Finsterwalder, 2016).

One of the most important consequences of the misuse of available resources in service systems is value co-contamination (Williams, Kang, & Johnson, 2016). In fact, when the providers and the users are not able to match their mutual expectations and to recognize their individual contribution to the appropriate functioning of the service system, a significant risk of value depreciation arises, which is rooted in the absence of a common understanding of the value concepts underlying the process of service provision. As a consequence, value co-creation is prevented; quite the opposite, the conflicting perspectives brought by the providers and the users result in value co-destruction dynamics.

Focusing the attention on user-provider relationships, Echeverri and Skålén (2011) depicted five recurring interaction value practices, which could be characterized by either co-creation or co-destruction dynamics. These five interactions practices concern the various stages of user-provider relationships, including: informing, greeting, delivering, charging, and helping. Informing is the first step to user engagement and—consequently—to service co-production. Indeed, the providers perform as the key sources of information for the users, which allow to improve the latter awareness of their co-production potential and to encourage their active involvement in value co-creation. Greeting is the initial point of contact between the users and the providers. This is a crucial phase, since it addresses the development of the co-creating relationship and is able to influence the users' willingness to factually participate in service co-production. Delivering is the core phase of user-provider co-creating relationship: both the users and the providers have the opportunity to express their contribution in the process of value creation, being concomitantly engaged in the service design and delivery. Charging concludes the exchange relationship between the two parties, consisting of a quantification of the value which has been created during the service encounter. Last but not least, helping involves a perpetuation of the user-provider relationship beyond

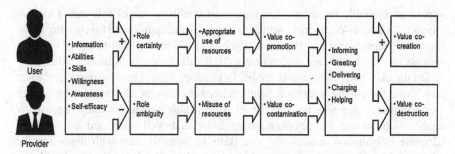

Fig. 3.2 Value co-destruction dynamics in service systems. *Source* Author's elaboration

the delivery process, in a perspective of enhanced value co-creation. Obviously, for each of these interaction practices the activation of value co-creation or co-destruction processes relies on the perspectives, inputs, and expectations brought by the users and the providers during the service encounter.

Figure 3.2 provides a graphical synthesis of the antecedents of value co-destruction relationships. Role ambiguity could be argued to perform as the most significant determinant of co-destroying relationships between the users and the providers. In fact, role ambiguity itself paves the way for increased risks of resource misuse during the user-provider encounter. On the one hand, resource misuse directly affect value co-creation dynamics; on the other hand, it produces value co-contamination risks, which may amplify value co-destruction. Drawing on the conceptual framework suggested by Echeverri and Skålén (2011), such co-destroying practices may happen at different points of contact between the users and the providers, with unavoidable drawbacks on the well-being of both of them. In light of these arguments, the next section discusses the risks of value co-destruction in the peculiar healthcare delivery systems, investigating under which circumstances the patients and the healthcare professionals may perform as value co-destroyers rather than as partners in the delivery of health services.

3.3 Patients and Healthcare Professionals as Value Co-destroyers

Taking inspiration from the SD logic perspective, it is possible that patient empowerment initiatives—as well as the related activation of enhanced relationships between the patients and the healthcare professionals—may pave the way for value co-destruction, rather than for value co-creation (Palumbo, 2015b). Sticking to what has been discussed in the previous section, it is especially likely that in the healthcare service system the patients and the providers of care participate in co-planning, co-designing and co-delivering health services by bringing contrasting expectations, conflicting inputs and diverging ends (Joos & Hickam, 1990). In turn, this situation determines role ambiguity and uncertainty, which entail increased likelihood of misuse of available resources. The misuse of health resources activates a vicious process of value co-destruction, which undermines the appropriate functioning of the healthcare service system (Palumbo, 2017) and affects the well-being of both the patients and the healthcare professionals (Helkkula, Linna, & Kelleher, 2013).

On the one hand, the patients are likely to adopt a first person perspective when they strive for coping with their health-related conditions. However, even though they intimately perceive the decline of their health conditions, they are usually unable to point out the determinants of individual well-being and do not have adequate information, knowledge and skills to properly deal with them. On the other hand, embracing the traditional bio-medical approach to care, the healthcare professionals are used to endorse a third person point of view during the medical encounter and to adopt a technical and reductionist perspective to cope with health-related issues. In addition, the healthcare professionals have usually adequate information about the determinants of the illness, as well as appropriate knowledge and skills to make timely and appropriate health-related decisions. From this standpoint, the conflicting expectations and perceptions of the patients and the healthcare professionals, which are influenced by their different perspectives, may prevent the establishment of a co-creating partnership, producing contrasting behaviors (Zoffmann & Kirkevold, 2005).

Since they adopt an external interpretation of the disease, the healthcare providers are likely to stick to the traditional biomedical approach to care, in an attempt to preserve their control over health-related decisions (Weller, Baer, de Alba Garcia, & Salcedo Rocha, 2012). Alternatively, the willingness of the patients to be involved in the provision of care may be frustrated by their condition of information asymmetry and psychological dependence, which do not allow patient enablement and activation (Aujoulat, Luminet, & Deccache, 2007). As a consequence, the conflicting propositions of the patients and the healthcare providers may lead to the emergence of an anti-service mentality, which deeply influences the process of value co-creation (Hill & Hill, 2015). What is even more interesting, is that the emergence of an anti-service mentality may lead toward patient disengagement, since it discourages the patients to awaken and use their sleeping resources for the purposes of health protection and promotion (Aujoulat, Marcolongo, Bonadiman, & Deccache, 2008).

Adhering to the assumption that patient empowerment initiatives produce a radical shift in the role and expectations of both the patients and the providers, scholars have identified several critical areas which should be properly managed in order to minimize the risks of value co-destruction in the healthcare service system (Osei-Frimpong, Wilson, & Owusu-Frimpong, 2015). These critical areas include: (1) the specific behaviors and the attitudes of the patients and the healthcare professionals; (2) the attributes of the co-creating partnership which is built between them; and (3) the social context in which such a partnership is established.

The greater the ability of the patients and the healthcare providers to build a positive attitude toward patient empowerment and to enhance the social context in which their partnership is built, the higher their role certainty and—consequently— the greater the opportunities for value co-creation (Annarumma & Palumbo, 2016). On the opposite, if the healthcare professionals are unable and/or unwilling to enhance the meaningfulness of the social context in which their encounter with the patients takes place and the patients are unable to develop positive attitudes and beliefs toward the process of empowerment (Palumbo, Annarumma, Musella, & Adinolfi, 2016b), role ambiguity arises, determining significant risks of value co-destruction (Deber, 1994).

Echoing these considerations, Naaranoja and Uden (2014) pointed out that value co-creation in the healthcare service system may be prevented by the poor ability of the patients and the healthcare professionals to disclose their mutual expectations. Besides, they may unable to share their knowledge and information in order to achieve a common understanding of their respective contribution to the protection and the promotion of the individual well-being. Since the patients and the healthcare professionals are likely to adopt different interpretative pathways to grasp with the illness and to guide their behaviors during the medical encounter, the exchange of information and knowledge is at risk of being biased, strengthening the condition of information asymmetry and the patients' dependence on the providers of care (Barile, Saviano, & Polese, 2014). As anticipated above, the healthcare professionals are used to interpret health-related issues according to a rational model, which is bases on procedures and protocols; alternatively, the patients are primarily influenced by values and emotions in realizing their choices in the healthcare environment. If the clash between these two different perspectives is not edged, the patients and the healthcare providers activate a process of value co-contamination, which triggers a co-destruction dynamic.

One of the most important by-products of the biased patient-provider relationship is the limited interest of the healthcare professionals to interact with empowered patients. In fact, the healthcare professionals may perceive a tension between their sense of professional responsibility and the involvement of the patients in the design and delivery of care, which implies a shift in the control over health-related decisions (Wilson & Mayor, 2006). To avoid the loss of power, the healthcare professionals may strive for increasing their control over the interaction practices with their patients. In other words, the healthcare professionals may attempt to preserve their medical dominance over the patients, transforming patient empowerment initiatives into restrictions of the patients' autonomy and freedom of choice (Wilson, Kendall, & Brooks, 2007).

As discussed in the Second Chapter, digital tools and information and communication technologies may be used as crucial instruments to bridge the gap between the healthcare professionals and the patients. In fact, they create a virtual space which foster mutual interactions and support information and knowledge sharing (Alpay, Henkemans, Otten, Rövekamp, & Dumay, 2010). However, it is possible that digital tools further unbalance the relationship between the patients and the healthcare providers, paving the way for increased risks of value co-destruction. In particular, information and communication technologies assign a greater control over health decisions to the patients, who are expected to be able to deal with health issues (Lemire, 2010). People living with inadequate health-related competencies may misuse the digital resources, being unable to adequately use them for the purposes of health protection and promotion (Robertson, Polonsky, &

McQuilken, 2014). In this circumstance, the use of information technologies to mediate the relationship between the patients and the healthcare providers could be itself a determinant of value co-destruction, due to either the inadequate skills of the patients or the poor friendliness of information provided through digital tools. From this point of view, in order to avoid the occurrence of value co-destruction, it is critical that the healthcare professionals assist the patients in properly accessing and using health-related information retrieved from information and communication technologies (Schulz & Nakamoto, 2013).

In sum, it is possible that the empowerment of the patients and their involvement in co-planning, co-designing and co-delivering health services may produce negative drawbacks on the patient-provider relationship. On the one hand, the healthcare professionals may feel threatened by patient empowerment, being afraid of losing their control over health-related issues. On the other hand, the patients may be unaware of what they are required to do in order to perform as value co-creators in the healthcare environment, being at risk of establishing biased relationships with the providers of care. Implementing patient empowerment initiatives without taking into considerations the ability and the willingness of both patients and healthcare professionals to establish a co-creating relationship may pave the way for value co-destruction, which negatively affects the proper functioning of the healthcare service system.

3.4   The Need for Enlightening and Managing the Dark Side of Patient Empowerment

Patient empowerment implies a radical shift in the relationship between the patients and the healthcare professionals. They are encouraged to enter in a partnership, which is ultimately intended to improve the quality of the medical encounter and to enhance the health outcomes achievable (van Dam, van der Horst, van den Borne, Ryckman, & Crebolder, 2003). Echoing these considerations, scholars and practitioners have focused most of their attention on the positive consequences which could be attached to patient empowerment. In particular, the enablement of the patients' sleeping resources and their activation for the purposes of health protection and promotion has been related to the achievement of a balance of power between the healthcare professionals and the patients; as well, it leads toward patient involvement in health-related decision making and health services' delivery (Fischer, 2014). Alternatively, little attention has been paid to the dark side of patient empowerment (Palumbo, 2015a). In other words, the scientific literature has stressed the value added of patient empowerment initiatives, while the risks of value co-destruction in the healthcare service system have been overlooked both in conceptual and in practical terms (Robertson, Polonsky, & McQuilken, 2014). Nonetheless, the clash between the process of patient empowerment and the healthcare professionals' autonomy may pave the way for the emergence of conflicting perspectives and diverging aims (Erlingsdóttir & Lindholm, 2015), which in turn prevent value co-creation in co-designing and co-delivering health services (Palumbo, 2016b).

For the sake of the argument, the healthcare professionals may conceive patient empowerment initiatives as a sort of constrained collaboration, which is not consistent with the key tenets of the traditional biomedical approach to care and limits the healthcare providers' autonomy in devising an appropriate treatment to cope with the disease (Vinson, 2016). At the same time, the patients may feel unconfident in navigating the healthcare service system; therefore, they could be unwilling to actively participate in the provision of care as value co-creators (Seale et al., 2015). In this circumstance, the establishment of enhanced patient-provider relationship is expected to produce increased risks of resource misuse and, consequently, value co-destruction.

In order to edge the rise of value co-destruction in the patient-provider relationship and to encourage the patients and the healthcare professionals to jointly participate in health services' co-production, the dark side of patient empowerment should be enlightened and handled. In an attempt to delve into this issue, the next and concluding Chapter focus the attention on health literacy, a dynamic and multi-faceted concept which is strictly related to patient empowerment. In particular, health literacy plays a crucial role in shedding light on the dark side of patient empowerment, being conceived as a fundamental ingredient of the recipe for increased patient involvement in the provision of care.

A dual interpretation of health literacy will be used, which echoes the relational interpretation of patient empowerment. Individual health literacy concerns the patients' ability to be engaged in co-planning, co-designing and co-delivering healthcare services. Organizational health literacy involves the readiness of the healthcare professionals to empower the patients and to encourage their active engagement in value co-creation activities. Both individual and organizational health literacy concur in preventing the emergence of value co-destruction in the healthcare delivery system, setting the conditions for the establishment of a vivid co-creating partnership between the patients and the providers of care.

References

Adinolfi, P., Starace, F., & Palumbo, R. (2016). Health outcomes and patient empowerment. The case of health budgets in Italy. *Journal of Health Management, 18*(1), 117–133.

Alpay, L. L., Henkemans, O. B., Otten, W., Rövekamp, T. A., & Dumay, A. C. (2010). E-health applications and services for patient empowerment: Directions for best practices in the Netherlands. *Telemedicine and e-Health, 16*(7), 787–791.

Alper, J. (2015). *Health literacy: Past, present, and future. Workshop summary.* Washington D.C.: The National Academy Press.

Anderson, R. M., & Funnell, M. M. (2005). Patient empowerment: Reflections on the challenge of fostering the adoption of a new paradigm. *Patient Education and Counselling, 57*(2), 153–157.

Annarumma, C., & Palumbo, R. (2016). Contextualizing health literacy to health care organizations: Exploratory insights. *Journal of Health Management, 18*(4), 611–624.

Aujoulat, I., d'Hoore, W., & Deccache, A. (2007a). Patient empowerment in theory and practice: Polysemy or cacophony? *Patient Education and Counseling, 66*(1), 13–20.

Aujoulat, I., Luminet, O., & Deccache, A. (2007b). The perspective of patients on their experience of powerlessness. *Qualitative Health Research, 17*(6), 772–785.

Aujoulat, I., Marcolongo, R., Bonadiman, L., & Deccache, A. (2008). Reconsidering patient empowerment in chronic illness: A critique of models of self-efficacy and bodily control. *Social Science and Medicine, 66*(5), 1228–1239.

Barile, S., Saviano, M., & Polese, F. (2014). Information asymmetry and co-creation in health care services. *Australasian Marketing Journal, 22*(3), 205–217.

Bee, P., Price, O., Baker, J., & Lovell, K. (2015). Systematic synthesis of barriers and facilitators to service user-led care planning. *The British Journal of Psychiatry, 207*(2), 104–114.

Bion, J. F., & Heffner, J. E. (2004). Challenges in the care of the acutely ill. *The Lancet, 363* (9413), 970–977.

Brach, C., Dreyer, B. P., & Schillinger, D. (2014). Physicians' roles in creating health literate organizations: A call to action. *Journal of General Internal Medicine, 29*(2), 273–275.

Bridges, J. F. P., Loukanova, S., & Carrera, P. (2009). Patient empowerment in health care. In G. Carrin, K. Buse, K. Heggenhougen, & S. R. Quah (Eds.), *Health systems policy, finance, and organization* (pp. 370–380). Oxford: Academic Press.

Callaway, S. K., & Dobrzykowski, D. D. (2009). Service-oriented entrepreneurship: Service-dominant logic in green design and healthcare. *Service Science, 1*(4), 225–240.

Camacho, N., Landman, V., & Stremersch, S. (2010). The Connected Patients. In S. Wuyts, M. Dekimpe, E. Gijsbrechts, & R. Pieters (Eds.), *The connected customer: The changing nature of consumer and business markets* (pp. 107–139). New York: Taylor & Francis.

Chan, K. W., Yim, C. K., & Lam, S. S. (2010). Is customer participation in value creation a double-edged sword? evidence from professional financial services across cultures. *Journal of Marketing, 74*(3), 48–64.

Ciasullo, M. V., Palumbo, R., & Troisi, O. (2017). Reading public service co-production through the lenses of requisite variety. *International Journal of Business and Management, 12*(2), 1–13.

Coburn, D. (2006). Medical dominance then and now: Critical reflections. *Health Sociology Review, 15*(5), 432–443.

Covolo, L., Rubinelli, S., Orizio, G., & Gelatti, U. (2012). Misuse (and abuse?) of the concept of empowerment. The case of online offer of predictive direct-to-consumer genetic tests. *Journal of Public Health Research, 1*(e3), 7–10.

Deber, R. B. (1994). The patient-physician partnership: Changing roles and the desire for information. *Canadian Medical Association Journal, 151*(2), 171–176.

Echeverri, P., & Skålén, P. (2011). Co-creation and co-destruction: A practice-theory based study of interactive value formation. *Marketing Theory, 11*(3), 351–373.

Edvardsson, B., Tronvoll, B., & Gruber, T. (2011). Expanding understanding of service exchange and value co-creation: A social construction approach. *Journal of the Academy of Marketing Science, 39*(2), 327–339.

Erlingsdóttir, G., & Lindholm, C. (2015). When patient empowerment encounters professional autonomy: The conflict and negotiation process of inscribing an eHealth service. *Scandinavian Journal of Public Administration, 19*(2), 27–48.

Faulkner, M. (2001). Empowerment and disempowerment: Models of staff/patient interaction. *NT Research, 6*(6), 936–948.

Fischer, S. (2014). Patient choice and consumerism in healthcare: Only a mirage of wishful thinking? An essay on theoretical and empirical aspects. In S. Gurtner & K. Soyez (Eds.), *Challenges and opportunities in health care management* (pp. 173–184). Cham: Springer International Publishing.

Fraenkel, L., & McGraw, S. (2007). What are the essential elements to enable patient participation in medical decision making? *Journal of General Internal Medicine, 22*(5), 614–619.

French, M., & Hernandez, L. (2013). *Organizational change to improve health literacy: Workshop summary.* Washington, DC: National Academies Press.

Gibson, C. H. (1991). A concept analysis of empowerment. *Journal of Advanced Nursing, 16*(3), 354–361.

Gill, L., White, L., & Cameron, I. D. (2011). Service co-creation in community-based aged healthcare. *Managing Service Quality: An International Journal, 21*(2), 152–177.

Grönroos, C., & Ravald, A. (2011). Service as business logic: Implications for value creation and marketing. *Journal of Service Management, 22*(1), 5–22.

Haidet, P., Kroll, T. L., & Sharf, B. F. (2006). The complexity of patient participation: Lessons learned from patients' illness narratives. *Patient Education and Counseling, 62*(3), 323–329.

Hardyman, W., Daunt, K. L., & Kitchener, M. (2015). Value cocreation through patient engagement in health care: A micro-level approach and research agenda. *Public Management Review, 17*(1), 90–107.

Helkkula, A., Linna, M., & Kelleher, C. (2013). Health, cost, prevention and cure—value and value co-creation in public healthcare. In E. Gummesson, C. Mele & F. Polese (Eds.), *Service dominant logic, network and systems theory and service science: Integrating three perspectives for a new service agenda, Naples* (pp. 1–20).

Hill, P., & Hill, R. (2015). Antiservice and healthcare consumers: A tale of two environments. In K. Diehl & C. Yoon (Eds.), *Association for consumer research, Duluth, MN* (pp. 555–556).

Joos, S. K., & Hickam, D. H. (1990). How health professionals influence health behavior: Patient-provider interaction and health care outcomes. In K. Glanz, F. M. Lewis, & B. K. Rimer (Eds.), *Health behavior and health education: Theory, research, and practice* (pp. 216–241). San Francisco, CA: Jossey-Bass.

Koh, H. K., Baur, C., Brach, C., Harris, L. M., & Rowden, J. N. (2013). Toward a systems approach to health literacy research. *Journal of Health Communication, 18*(1), 1–5.

Kuppelwieser, V. G., & Finsterwalder, J. (2016). Transformative service research and service dominant logic: Quo Vaditis? *Journal of Retailing and Consumer Services, 28,* 91–98.

Lemire, M. (2010). What can be expected of information and communication technologies in terms of patient empowerment in health? *Journal of Health Organization and Management, 24*(2), 167–181.

Lindberg, C., Sivberg, B., Willman, A., & Fagerström, C. (2015). A trajectory towards partnership in care—Patient experiences of autonomy in intensive care: A qualitative study. *Intensive & Critical Care Nursing, 31*(5), 294–302.

McAllister, M., Dunn, G., Payne, K., Davies, L., & Todd, C. (2012). Patient empowerment: The need to consider it as a measurable patient-reported outcome for chronic conditions. *BMC Health Services Research, 12*(157), doi:10.1186/1472-6963-12-157

McWilliam, C. L., Brown, J. B., Carmichael, J. L., & Lehman, J. M. (1994). A new perspective on threatened autonomy in elderly persons: The disempowering process. *Social Science and Medicine, 38*(2), 327–338.

Merz, M. Y., Czerwinski, D., & Merz, M. A. (2013). Exploring the antecedents for value co-creation during healthcare service provision. *Journal of Business and Behavior Sciences, 25*(2), 152–166.

Naaranoja, M., & Uden, L. (2014). Why co-creation of value may not work? In L. Uden, D. F. Oshee, I.-H. Ting, & D. Liberona (Eds.), *Knowledge management in organizations* (pp. 362–372). Cham: Springer International Publishing.

O'Neal, K. S., Crosby, K. M., Miller, M. J., Murray, K. A., & Condren, M. E. (2013). Assessing health literacy practices in a community pharmacy environment: Experiences using the AHRQ pharmacy health literacy assessment tool. *Administrative Pharmacy, 9*(5), 564–596.

Örtqvist, D., & Wincent, J. (2006). Prominent consequences of role stress: A meta-analytic review. *International Journal of Stress Management, 13*(4), 399–411.

Osei-Frimpong, K., Wilson, A., & Owusu-Frimpong, N. (2015). Service experiences and dyadic value co-creation in healthcare service delivery: A CIT approach. *Journal of Service Theory and Practice, 25*(4), 443–462.

Ouschan, R., Sweeney, J., & Johnson, L. (2003). The dimensions of patient empowerment: A chronic illness consultations perspective. In J. E. Lewin (Ed.), *World Marketing Congress—Academy of Marketing Science, Perth, WA.*

Palumbo, R. (2015a). The dark side of health care co-production. Health literacy as a requisite for the co-production of care. *International Journal of Social Science & Human Behavior Study, 2*(1), 82–86.

Palumbo, R. (2015b). Value co-creation and value co-destruction in the patient-provider relationship. The contribution of the "Health Literacy" perspective. In V. Demetris, W. Yaakov & T. Evangelos (Eds.), *Innovation, Entrepreneurship and Sustainable Value Chain in a Dynamic Environment* (pp. 1266–1279). Verona: 8th Euromed Annual Conference.

Palumbo, R. (2016a). Designing health-literate health care organization: A literature review. *Health Services Management Research, 29*(3), 79–87.

Palumbo, R. (2016b). Contextualizing co-production of health care: A systematic literature review. *International Journal of Public Sector Management, 29*(1), 72–90.

Palumbo, R. (2017). Toward a new conceptualization of health care services to inspire public health. Public national health service as a "common pool of resources". *International review on Public and Nonprofit Marketing*. Published online ahead of print. doi:10.1007/s12208-017-0175-1

Palumbo, R., Annarumma, C., Musella, M., Adinolfi, P., & Piscopo, G. (2016a). The italian health literacy project: Insights from the assessment of health literacy skills in Italy. *Health Policy, 120*(9), 1087–1094.

Palumbo, R., Annarumma, C., Musella, M., & Adinolfi, P. (2016b). Examining the meaningfulness of healthcare organizations in the light of patient empowerment. *Academy of Management Proceedings, 1*(12315). doi:10.5465/AMBPP.2016.12315abstract

Patton, D. (2013). Strategic direction or operational confusion: level of service user involvement in Irish acute admission uñit care. *Journal of Psychiatric and Mental Health Nursing, 20*(5), 387–395.

Plé, L., & Cáceres, R. C. (2010). Not always co-creation: Introducing interactional co-destruction of value in service-dominant logic. *Journal of Services Marketing, 24*(6), 430–437.

Prahalad, C., & Ramaswamy, V. (2004). *The future of competition: Co-creating unique value with customers.* Boston, MA: Harvard Business School Press.

Prigge, J.-K., Dietz, B., Homburg, C., Hoyer, W. D., & Burton, J. L. (2015). Patient empowerment: A cross-disease exploration of antecedents and consequences. *International Journal of Research in Marketing, 32*(4), 375–386.

Robertson, N., Polonsky, M., & McQuilken, L. (2014). Are my symptoms serious Dr Google? A resource-based typology of value co-destruction in online self-diagnosis. *Australasian Marketing Journal, 22*(3), 246–256.

Rogers, B., & Dunne, E. (2013). A qualitative study on the use of the care programme approach with individuals with borderline personality disorder: A service user perspective. *Journal of Psychosocial Nursing and Mental Health Services, 51*(10), 38–45.

Ryan, J., & Sysko, J. (2007). The contingency of patient preferences for involvement in health decision making. *Health Care Management Review, 32*(1), 30–36.

Salmon, P., & Hall, G. (2003). Patient empowerment and control: A psychological discourse in the service of medicine. *Social Science and Medicine, 57*(10), 1969–1980.

Salmon, P., & Hall, G. M. (2004). Patient empowerment or the emperor's new clothes. *Journal of the Royal Society of Medicine, 97*(2), 53–56.

Santana, S., Lausen, B., Bujnowska-Fedak, M., Chronaki, C. E., Prokosch, H.-U., & Wynn, R. (2011). Informed citizen and empowered citizen in health: Results from an European survey. *BMC Family Practice, 12*(20). doi:10.1186/1471-2296-12-20

Schulz, P. J., & Nakamoto, K. (2013). Patient behavior and the benefits of artificial intelligence: The perils of "dangerous" literacy and illusory patient empowerment. *Patient Education and Counseling, 92*(2), 223–228.

Seale, H., Travaglia, J., Chughtai, A. A., Phillipson, L., Novytska, Y., & Kaur, R. (2015). 'I don't want to cause any trouble': The attitudes of hospital patients towards patient empowerment strategies to reduce healthcare-acquired infections. *Journal of Infection Prevention, 16*(4), 167–173.

Sjödin, D. R., Parida, V., & Wincent, J. (2016). Value co-creation process of integrated product-services: Effect of role ambiguities and relational coping strategies. *Industrial Marketing Management, 56,* 108–119.

Smith, A. M. (2013). The value co-destruction process: A customer resource perspective. *European Journal of Marketing* (47), 1889–1909.

Sweeney, J. C. (2007). Moving towards the service-dominant logic—a comment. *Australasian Marketing Journal, 15*(1), 97–104.

Tritter, J. Q., & McCallum, A. (2006). The snakes and ladders of user involvement: Moving beyond Arnstein. *Health Policy, 76*(2), 156–168.

van Dam, H. A., van der Horst, F., van den Borne, B., Ryckman, R., & Crebolder, H. (2003). Provider–patient interaction in diabetes care: Effects on patient self-care and outcomes: A systematic review. *Patient Education and Counseling, 51*(1), 17–28.

Vargo, S. L., Maglio, P. P., & Akaka, M. A. (2008). On value and value co-creation: A service systems and service logic perspective. *European Management Journal, 26*(3), 145–152.

Vinson, A. H. (2016). 'Constrained collaboration': Patient empowerment discourse as resource for countervailing power. *Sociology of Health & Illness, 38*(8), 1364–1378.

Weaver, N. L., Wray, R. J., Zellin, S., Gautam, K., & Jupka, K. (2012). Advancing organizational health literacy in health care organizations serving high-needs populations: A case study. *Journal of Health Communication, 17*(S3), 55–66.

Weller, S. C., Baer, R. D., de Alba Garcia, J. G., & Salcedo Rocha, A. L. (2012). Explanatory models of diabetes in the U.S. and Mexico: The patient–provider gap and cultural competence. *Social Science & Medicine, 75*(6), 1088–1096.

Williams, B. N., Kang, S.-C., & Johnson, J. (2016). (Co)-Contamination as the dark side of co-production: Public value failures in co-production processes. *Public Management Review, 18*(5), 692–717.

Wilson, P. M., Kendall, S., & Brooks, F. (2007). The expert patients programme: A paradox of patient empowerment and medical dominance. *Health and Social Care in the Community, 15*(5), 426–438.

Wilson, P., & Mayor, V. (2006). Long-term conditions. Supporting and enabling self-care. *British Journal of Community Nursing, 11*(1), 6–10.

Zoffmann, V., & Kirkevold, M. (2005). Life versus disease in difficult diabetes care: Conflicting perspectives disempower patients and professionals in problem solving. *Qualitative Health Research, 15*(6), 750–765.

Chapter 4
The Role of Health Literacy in Empowering Patients

4.1 The Different Shades of Health Literacy

As discussed in the previous sections of this brief, patient-centeredness and patient empowerment are expected to deeply affect the shapes of the healthcare system of the future. However, several scholars have pointed out that, when they access health services, the patients may be unwilling to enter in a co-creating partnership with the healthcare professionals (Thompson, 2007). At the same time, it has been reported that the healthcare professionals may face some hurdles when they strive for building cooperative relationships with the patients in the attempt to engage them in the provision of care (Zanini et al., 2015). As a consequence, a bio-medical approach to care arises, which is based on professional dominance.

What is even more interesting, is that there is still poor agreement on the individual and organizational factors which could either foster or prevent the process of patient empowerment (Barello, Graffigna, & Vegni, 2012). Among others, the patients' inadequate ability to handle health information, to deal with health-related issues and to navigate the healthcare system—that is to say, limited individual health literacy (Berkman, Davis, & McCormack, 2010)—and the problematic ability of healthcare organizations to establish a clear and comfortable relationship with the patients—that is to say limited organizational health literacy (Palumbo, 2016)—have been argued to pave the way for biased patient-provider relations. In other words, limited health literacy—at both the individual and the organizational levels—has been considered to be able to hinder the engagement and the involvement of the patients in the delivery of care, thus preventing value co-creation in the healthcare service system (Hasnain-Wynia & Wolf, 2010). From this point of view, a focus on health literacy is strongly needed in order to better contextualize patient empowerment initiatives.

Health literacy is a multifaceted and dynamic concept, which is composed of different shades. This construct was formerly introduced in early 70s by Simonds (1974), who conceived it as a fundamental issue in social policy. Sticking to these

© The Author(s) 2017
P. Rocco, *The Bright Side and the Dark Side of Patient Empowerment*,
SpringerBriefs in Public Health, DOI 10.1007/978-3-319-58344-0_4

propositions, health literacy is crucial to bridge the gap between education and health. Indeed, it is argued to enhance the individual ability to cope with the disease and to navigate the healthcare service system. Drawing on these arguments, health literacy has been initially associated with the inclusion of mandatory topics in the field of health protection and promotion within all school grade levels education programs, in order to arise the pupils' awareness of health-related issues and improve their ability to deal with them.

It is evident that this original conceptualization of health literacy was derived from a functional interpretation (Baker et al., 1999). In other words, health literacy was understood as the personal ability to access, process, understand, and use health information at a level adequate to properly function within the healthcare environment and to perform basic tasks to cope with the illness (Parker et al., 1995). Embracing such a functional perspective, health literacy could be represented as a one-way street, which solely concerns the patients' ability to understand health information materials and to properly use them in order to navigate the healthcare service system.

A few decades later, Nutbeam (2008) proposed an alternative interpretation of health literacy, claiming that—beyond functional competencies—interactive and critical skills contribute in enhancing the individual ability to handle health-related issues. On the one hand, health literacy involves the ability to build and maintain clear and meaningful relationships with the different sources of health information which operate within the healthcare environment, including the providers of care (Parmer et al., 2015). On the other hand, health literate patients are considered to be proficient in discriminating within the health information available, in order to make timely and effective decisions to cope with the disease (Sykes et al., 2013). In light of these propositions, three sets of health-related competencies are argued to simultaneously build the health literacy construct: functional health literacy (Williams et al., 1998), interactive health literacy (Rubin et al., 2011) and critical health literacy (Chinn, 2011). Ultimately, as depicted in Table 4.1, individual health literacy is based on three different kinds of health-related skills: functional, interactive, and critical competences.

Table 4.1 The three building blocks of health literacy (HL)

HL Skill	Description	Contribution to PE
Functional HL	Basic skills required to obtain, read, understand and process health-related information	Functional HL is critical to enable and activate the patients' sleeping resources
Interactive HL	Intermediate social skills required to establish meaningful relationship within the healthcare service system	Interactive HL fosters patient engagement and involvement in the provision of care
Critical HL	Advanced skills to make informed health decisions during everyday life contingencies	Critical HL entails a full-fledged patient empowerment and leads to shared decision making

Source Author's elaboration

Merging the functional, interactive and critical shades at the basis of this construct, health literacy turns out to be a complex set of skills which are required to improve the individual ability to handle health-related issues and to identify and select the best alternatives available to protect and promote the psycho-physical well-being (Baker, 2006). From this point of view, adequate health literacy has been variously found to be crucial to achieve patient engagement (Coulter, 2012). Alternatively, people living with limited health literacy skills have been reported to be more likely to escape patient involvement (Williams et al., 2002). In particular, limited health literacy has been argued to produce shame and stigma from the side of patients, which in turn discourage their active engagement in the provision of care (Parikh et al., 1996). Therefore, it could be maintained that adequate individual health literacy is an important ingredient of the recipe for increased patient participation in the design and delivery of care.

In most of the cases, limited health literacy has been discussed as a personal fault of the patients (Palumbo, 2015). Alternatively, it has been rarely presented as a potential flaw of the healthcare service system (French & Hernandez, 2013). However, in recent years the scientific literature pointed out that health services are usually designed by assuming limitless health literacy skills of the patients (Brach et al., 2012). That is to say, healthcare settings are arranged without taking into consideration the patients' health literacy skills, thus producing significant risks of inappropriate access to care and inadequate use of health resources available. Hence, it is likely that the inadequate health-related skills of those who live with problematic health literacy are compounded by the complexity of the healthcare environment (Weaver et al., 2012). The greater the gap between the patients' health literacy skills and the friendliness of the healthcare environment, the higher the risks of confusion and misunderstanding by the side of patients, which pave the way for patient disempowerment and disengagement from the provision of health services.

Organizational health literacy involves an attempt to bridge the gap between the patients and the healthcare organizations, promoting a clear exchange of information and encouraging the establishment of a co-creating partnership which is consistent with a patient-centered approach to care. Indeed, it involves a full involvement of the patients in health services' design and delivery, emphasizing the need for putting the patient at the heart of the healthcare system (Brach, Dreyer, & Schillinger, 2014). Obviously, the greater the organizational health literacy of healthcare organizations, the better their ability to empower the patients and to engage them in a long-term partnership intended to value co-creation (Annarumma & Palumbo, 2016).

Summarizing, patient empowerment may be argued to rely on both individual and organizational health literacy. Figure 4.1 depicts the interplay between these two variables, positioning patient empowerment at the intersection between individual and organizational health literacy. In spite of what has been discussed above, scholars are still not consistent in discussing the consequences of inadequate

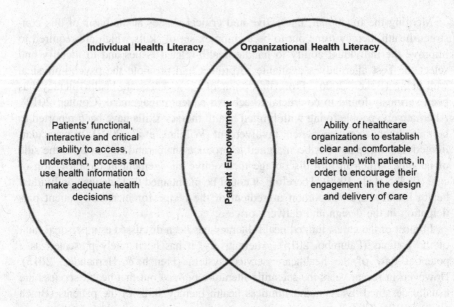

Fig. 4.1 The interplay between individual and organizational health literacy. *Source* Author's elaboration

individual and organizational health literacy on patient empowerment initiatives (Palumbo et al., 2016b). Therefore, further conceptual and empirical developments are required to shed light on this crucial issue.

4.2 Disentangling the Relationship Between Individual Health Literacy and Patient Empowerment

Limited individual health literacy has been depicted as a "silent epidemic" (Marcus, 2006, p. 339), which expresses significant drawbacks on the appropriate functioning of the healthcare service system. On the one hand, the literature is consistent in reporting the prevalence of problematic health literacy skills among the population served (Nielsen-Bohlman et al., 2004). For the sake of the argument, recent studies realized in Europe have shown that about 4 out of 10 people disclose a problematic ability to deal with health-related issues, reporting to meet significant barriers in navigating the healthcare system (Sørensen et al., 2015; Palumbo et al., 2016a). These data seem to echo the situation in the United States, where limited health literacy skills are prevailing (Paasche-Orlow et al., 2005). On the other hand, inadequate health literacy has been linked to the lower patients' willingness to participate in shared health decision making (Aboumatar et al., 2013); moreover, it is associated with a greater likelihood of shame perception by the side of patients

(Parikh et al., 1996) and increased risks of inappropriate access to care (Schumacher et al., 2013).

In light of these findings, a relationship between individual health literacy and patient empowerment could be pointed out. However, scholars and practitioners do not agree in disentangling the link between these two constructs. Among others, Schulz and Nakamoto (2013) emphasized the differences between health literacy and patient empowerment, presenting them as conjoined twins. In particular, even though health literacy and patient empowerment are considered to be strictly intertwined, they are argued to be uncorrelated. As a consequence, the potential discrepancy between health literacy skills and patient empowerment may produce negative consequences for the adequate functioning of the healthcare service system. Echoing Schulz and Nakamoto (2013, p. 4): "…*high levels of health literacy without a corresponding high degree of patient empowerment creates an unnecessary dependence of patients on health professionals*". Otherwise, "...*a high degree of empowerment without a corresponding degree of health literacy poses the risk of dangerous health choices*".

Drawing on these arguments, the effective involvement of patients in co-planning, co-designing and co-delivering health services concomitantly relies on both patient empowerment and health literacy. On the one hand, the lack of patient empowerment may produce dependent and vulnerable patients, who are not willing to partner with the healthcare professionals in order to actively participate in value co-creation, regardless of their functional, interactive and critical health-related competencies. On the other hand, the lack of adequate health literacy by the side of empowered patients entails higher risks on inappropriate health decisions and unhealthy behaviors, which are produced by the problematic ability of patients to access, understand, process and use health information (Camerini & Schulz, 2015).

Wang et al. (2016) revealed a more direct and strong relationship between health literacy and patient empowerment. In particular, it is pointed out that patient empowerment initiatives are at risk of being sterile when the patients do not show adequate functional, interactive and critical health-related competencies. Going more into details, the lower the individual health literacy skills, the poorer the patients' desire to be involved in self-care initiatives, regardless of the degree of patient empowerment. Sticking to these considerations, it could be claimed that health literacy is able to influence the process of patient empowerment, enhancing their ability to cope with health-related matters. At the same time, patient empowerment initiatives encourage a greater involvement of patients at the different stages of health services' design and delivery, thus contributing in the enhancement of their health literacy skills (McAllister, 2016). A positive and reinforcing cycle gets started, which emphasized the self-nourishing relationship between health literacy and patient empowerment.

Different variables have been reported to mediate the relationship between individual health literacy and patient empowerment. First of all, inadequate health literacy has been related to unmet information needs of the patients. Low health literate patients are likely to find difficulties in interacting with the healthcare professionals and understanding health information available (Halbach et al., 2016).

In turn, the impaired individual ability to handle health information is considered to prevent the process of patient empowerment, thus discouraging the patients' participation in the delivery of health services (Palumbo et al., 2016b). Moreover, problematic health literacy has been presented as a barrier which hinders the process of patient enablement and activation. The lower the patients' health literacy skills, the poorer their disease-related knowledge (Kim et al., 2001; Gazmararian et al., 2003) and, therefore, the lower their ability to identify and understand the determinants of the individual psycho-physical well-being (Williams et al., 1998). Echoing these arguments, it has been argued that inadequate health literacy may contaminate individual health beliefs, producing a biased cognitive framework which is able to hinder the engagement of the patients in health services' delivery (Federman et al., 2010).

Systematizing these points, individual health literacy performs as an important predictor of patient enablement, which—in turn—anticipates patient engagement and involvement (Smith et al., 2013). Adequate health literacy skills—especially interactive and critical ones—pave the way for a greater patients' awareness of health-related issues, as well as for an increased participation in self-care activities (Heijmans et al., 2015). Alternatively, problematic health literacy is associated with patient disengagement: it anticipates a lower patients' desire for participation in shared decision making and greater risks of decision uncertainty (McCaffery et al., 2013). Ultimately, the lack of adequate health literacy skills determines the patients' unawareness of health-related conditions and unwillingness to be involved in the provision of care, producing a sort of patient disempowerment (Mancuso & Rincon, 2006).

In spite of these considerations, health literacy has been widely overlooked when planning and implementing patient empowerment initiatives. From this point of view, health literacy could be depicted as a missing link to effective patient empowerment (Palumbo et al., 2016b). Figure 4.2 graphically summarizes the relationship between health literacy and patient empowerment, identifying the main variables which establish a bridge between these two constructs.

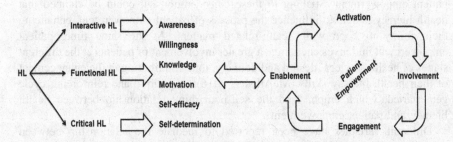

Fig. 4.2 The relationship between health literacy and patient empowerment. *Source* Author's elaboration

Individual health literacy involves the ability to access, obtain, process, understand and use written and oral health-related information; in addition, it encourages the establishment of a friendly and comfortable relationship with the providers of care. Last but not least, in concurs in the patients' capacity to discriminate within alternative health treatments available, in order to select the best option to cope with impaired health conditions. These three shades of individual health literacy—that is to say functional, interactive and critical health literacy—are key to awaken the patients' sleeping resources and to enable them for the purposes of health protection and promotion.

Adequate health literacy produces greater awareness of health-related issues, better knowledge of health determinants, higher willingness to participate in the delivery of care, stronger self-efficacy perception and greater desire to be engaged in health decision making. By virtue of these mediating variables, health literacy activates a self-nourishing cycle of patient empowerment, which is consistent with the factual implementation of a patient-centered approach to care. From this standpoint, the initiatives intended to promote individual health literacy skills turn out to be critical in order to empower the patients and to engage them in value co-creation within the healthcare environment.

4.3 Empowering Patients By Improving Individual Health Literacy

The previous paragraphs have stressed the critical role of individual health literacy in enabling the patients' sleeping resources and encouraging them to perform as value co-creators within the healthcare service system (Coulter, 2012; Palumbo, 2015). Even though the scientific interest in the field of health literacy has burgeoned since the last decades of the past century (Parker & Ratzan, 2010), there is still little evidence about the consequences on patient empowerment of the interventions which are aimed at enhancing the individual health literacy skills. Nonetheless, it could be maintained that the promotion of individual health literacy is a crucial step in the path toward patient empowerment. In fact, as reported by Sheridan et al. (2011), health literacy promotion interventions are able to increase the individual ability to navigate the healthcare environment, paving the way for: a more appropriate use of health services (Baker et al., 1998), lower disparities in the access to care (Bennett et al., 2009), and better health outcomes (Paasche-Orlow, 2011).

Scholars have suggested different taxonomies to categorize health literacy interventions. Taking into consideration the aims of these initiatives, DeWalt (2007) discriminated between four general types of health literacy interventions: (1) actions intended to improve the health literacy skills in the population; (2) actions intended to improve written and multimedia health communication; (3) actions intended to improve patient-provider communication; and (4) actions intended to alter the systems of care in a perspective of increased organizational health literacy. While the first three categories focus their attention on individual health literacy skills, the latter aims at increasing the ability of healthcare organizations to establish a friendly and comfortable relationship with the patients, removing the institutional, structural and cultural barriers which prevent patient involvement in the delivery of care (Palumbo, 2016).

Individual health education—in terms of both literacy and numeracy—and motivation are the main targets of the initiatives which are directed to the improvement of the health literacy skills in the population. In particular, these interventions attempt to increase the patients self-confidence to deal with health-related issues, as well as to enhance their willingness to participate in the provision of care (Manafo & Wong, 2012). Differently, print and on-line information materials are the primary interest of the interventions which are addressed to improve written and multimedia health communication: they should be understood as an effort to assist patients in collecting reliable and easy-to-understand information in order to effectively cope with the disease (Bryant et al., 2009). Last but not least, actions intended to improve patient-provider communication take place during the medical encounter and they are usually led by the healthcare professionals, who strive for encouraging the patients to play an active role in health decision making (Davis et al., 2008).

Drawing on Coulter and Ellins (2006), an alternative taxonomy of health literacy interventions could be proposed (D'Eath, Barry, & Sixsmith, 2012), which is based on the channels used to deliver these initiatives to the target population. From this point of view, four broad categories of health literacy interventions could be pointed out: (1) written health information interventions; (2) alternative format interventions; (3) tailored low-literacy initiatives; and (4) targeted mass-media campaigns.

Written health information interventions focus the attention on the patients' functional health literacy skills. They primarily aim at enhancing the accessibility and the readability of print materials, in order to help the patients in understanding and handling health information (Campbell et al., 2004). Therefore, written health information interventions focus on functional health literacy skills, assuming that the improvement of the patients' ability to access and use health information materials allows to increase their ability to navigate the healthcare service system and creates the conditions for patient empowerment.

Alternative format interventions entail the use of a wide array of health information beyond print materials, in an attempt to bridge the gap between education and health of low health literate patients. These initiatives strive for empowering the patients to perform self-care activities and to be involved in value co-creation (Gerber et al., 2005). For this purpose, they do not solely focus on functional health literacy; rather, they emphasize the importance of both interactive and critical skills to realize a full-fledged process of patient empowerment, which is rooted in greater self-confidence and self-effectiveness.

Tailored low-literacy initiatives are designed around the health needs of groups of low health literate people living with a particular disease and/or established in a specific geographical area. They are intended to increase the awareness of the health literacy resources available in the community, thus indirectly fostering patient empowerment (Sobel et al., 2009). In other words, these interventions are aimed at enabling the patients and increase the awareness of their contribution to the appropriate functioning of the healthcare service system.

Last but not least, targeted mass media campaigns do not concern particular groups of the target population which are identified on the basis of their health needs and/or diseases, but are designed around the promotion of specific healthy behaviours, such as the use of prevention services and health screening activities, in order to support the appropriate access to care (Volk et al., 2008). These interventions strive for putting into action the individual health literacy skills, paying a particular attention to interactive and critical skills.

In an attempt to synthesize these points, Clement et al. (2009) distinguished between simple and complex health literacy interventions. On the one hand, simple interventions consist of a single strategy to promote individual health literacy, such as the use of simplified written language, graphs, illustrations, and audio resources to improve the patients' capacity to delve into health information materials. Alternatively, complex interventions involve a mix of different health literacy promotion strategies, which are simultaneously aimed to improve the individual ability to navigate the healthcare service system. In most of the cases, all the elements of this mixed strategy seem to be essential to the effectiveness of the intervention; as a consequence, their main weakness could be retrieved in the difficulty to point out what is the active ingredient of the complex health literacy intervention.

In light of the prevailing focus on functional health literacy skills, it is not surprising the health literacy interventions generally adopts a simple strategy, in an attempt to improve the ability of the patients to access and use written health information materials, which in turn paves the way for increased disease-related knowledge and greater willingness to self-manage health-related conditions (Schaefer, 2008). However, even though the evidence on the outcomes of health literacy interventions is still variable (Berkman et al., 2011), it is worth noting that complex interventions have been argued to be more effective as compared with simple ones, being able to concomitantly affect health-related knowledge, self-care behaviors and health services' utilization (Barry, D'Eath, & Sixsmith, 2013). In addition, scholars have remarked that, to enhance the effectiveness of health literacy interventions, a specific attention to the context-specific social and cultural determinants of health literacy should be paid, in order to contextualize these initiatives and increase their potential impact (Dodson et al., 2015).

Figure 4.3 summarizes the above considerations about the characteristics and the effects on patient empowerment of health literacy interventions. Sticking to the multifaceted interpretation of the health literacy concept, complex interventions are argued to improve the different skills which are required to properly function within the healthcare environment. Traditional initiatives intended to increase the readability of print information materials and to assist the patients in understanding and using health information show a strict focus on functional health literacy. These actions should be complemented by the introduction of multimedia health communication, as well as by personalized initiatives, which enhance the

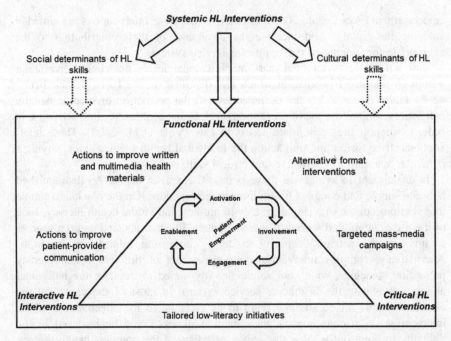

Fig. 4.3 The attributes and effects of complex health literacy interventions. *Source* Author's elaboration

patient-provider communication, in an effort to increase the individual interactive health-related competencies. Lastly, both tailored low-literacy initiatives and targeted mass-media campaigns allow to improve the individual critical health literacy skills, in order to increase the patients' awareness of their role within the healthcare service system and to encourage patient involvement. As anticipated, health literacy promotion initiatives should be supported by systemic actions, which contextualize health literacy interventions to the specific social and cultural determinants of patient empowerment within the target population.

4.4 The Way Forward to Patient Empowerment: Enhancing Organizational Health Literacy

It has been pointed out that health services are often designed assuming limitless health literacy skills of patients (Paasche-Orlow et al., 2006). As a consequence, there is a significant risk that patient empowerment initiatives result to be ineffective when they are addressed to people who live with problematic functional, interactive and critical health literacy skills. In addition, it is worth noting that health literacy has been usually approached according to an individualistic perspective, which focuses on the patients' ability to handle health information and to perform basic tasks within the healthcare environment (Berkman et al., 2010). Such a prevailing interpretation neglects that health literacy is a multi-faceted concept, which is the by-product of both the individual health-related competencies and the organizational attributes of the healthcare service system (Baker, 2006).

The organizational health literacy concept has been introduced in an attempt to recognize the critical role played by healthcare organizations in empowering the patients and in involving them in co-planning, co-designing and co-delivering health services (Koh et al., 2013). In spite of these considerations, several studies have shown that the healthcare organization are generally unaware of health literacy issues (Palumbo & Annarumma, 2016). What is even more interesting is that the healthcare organizations' contribution in promoting the health-related skills of the population served has been widely neglected both in theory and in practice (Weaver et al., 2012). To delve into this issue, greater attention should be paid to the ability of the healthcare organizations to activate the patients' sleeping resources and to encourage them to perform as value co-creators in the healthcare environment, rather than as mere consumers of health services (Willis et al., 2014).

As discussed in the First Chapter of this brief, Brach et al. (2012) identified ten attributes which are crucial to establish a health literate healthcare organization, which is considered to be able to identify and meet the patients' health-related needs. Going more into details, a health literate healthcare organization has been argued to: (1) rely on a group of leaders who make health literacy integral to the organizational mission, structures, and operations; (2) contemplate health literacy in its managerial actions, including planning, evaluation measures, patient safety, and quality improvement; (3) prepare its workforce to handle health literacy-related issues, raising the awareness of human resources of the consequences of inadequate health literacy on health outcomes; (4) engage the population served in the design, implementation, and evaluation of health information and health services; (5) meet the needs of the underserved population, overcoming stigma and shame associated with problematic health literacy; (6) use tailored health literacy strategies in interpersonal communications and confirms users' understanding at all points of contact between the patients and the providers of care; (7) provide the patients with easy to access health information and support them in navigating the healthcare service system; (8) design and distribute to patients print and audio-visual materials, as well as social media contents that are easy to use and to understand; (9) provide support to patients in high-risk situations, including care transitions and communications about medicines; and (10) communicate clearly what kind of services are covered by health plans and what kind of services should be paid out-of-pocket. Ultimately, a health literate healthcare organization is able to detect the patients' special information needs and strives for meeting them in an attempt to enhance the effectiveness of care (Livaudais-Toman et al., 2014). From this point of view, the link between organizational health literacy and patient empowerment is evident.

Interestingly, the scientific evidence on the ability of the healthcare organizations to deal with the specific needs of people living with problematic health literacy is scant. Notwithstanding, scholars are consistent in claiming the need for integrating health literacy issues in the design of healthcare organizations in order to realize a patient-centered approach to care (Briglia, Perlman, & Weissman, 2015). In particular, healthcare professionals have been argued to play a critical role in creating a health literate healthcare environment (Brach et al., 2014), since they have the opportunity to champion the organizational change and to foster the involvement of the patients in the design and delivery of care.

Supporting these arguments, recent developments have shown that the healthcare organizations are not likely to implement formal initiatives intended to enhance organizational health literacy. On the opposite, informal interventions led by healthcare professionals and aimed at inciting the patients to play an active role in health decision making and in the delivery of care seem to be more common. For the sake of the argument, the spontaneous support provided by healthcare providers to low health literate patients in navigating the healthcare system and the use of the teach back method and/or similar tools to enhance the patients' understanding of health information are key examples of informal initiatives to address organizational health literacy-related issues and to foster patient empowerment (Annarumma & Palumbo, 2016).

From this point of view, the commitment of the healthcare professionals turns out to be crucial to enhance organizational health literacy. The perspective of the healthcare organization staff about organizational health literacy-related issues could be investigated through three main conceptual domains, each of which deals with a specific shade of organizational health literacy: (1) the accessibility of print information materials; (2) the interpersonal communication between the healthcare professionals and the patients; and (3) sensitivity to health literacy issues (O'Neal et al., 2013).

On the one hand, it has been shown that healthcare professionals are aware of the role played by organizational health literacy in empowering the patients (Palumbo & Annarumma, 2016); on the other hand, the healthcare professionals are likely to find significant barriers in coping with the special information needs of people living with problematic health literacy, mainly due to the poor attention paid by healthcare organizations to the arrangement of clear verbal and written health information materials targeted to the understanding and processing skills of low health literate patients (Palumbo & Annarumma, 2016).

There is a strong need for further empirical research aimed at exploring how organizational health literacy contributes to the process of patient empowerment. Indeed, the healthcare organizations are in a critical position to enable the patients' sleeping resources and to encourage them to be actively involved in the design and delivery of care. The more health literate the healthcare organizations, the greater their ability to establish a co-creating partnership with the patients. Alternatively, inadequate organizational health literacy paves the way for the establishment of biased relationships between the patients and the healthcare professionals, which ultimately hinders the effectiveness of patient empowerment initiatives and prevent the patients themselves to perform as service co-producers in the healthcare service system.

References

Aboumatar, H. J., Carson, K. A., Beach, M. C., Roter, D. L., & Cooper, L. A. (2013). The impact of health literacy on desire for participation in healthcare, medical visit communication, and patient reported outcomes among patients with hypertension. *Journal of General Internal Medicine, 28*(11), 1469–1476.

Annarumma, C., & Palumbo, R. (2016). Contextualizing health literacy to health care organizations: Exploratory insights. *Journal of Health Management, 18*(4), 1–14.

Baker, D. W. (2006). The meaning and the measure of health literacy. *Journal of General Internal Medicine, 21*(8), 878–883.

Baker, D. W., Parker, R. M., Williams, M. V., & Clark, W. S. (1998). Health literacy and the risk of hospital admission. *Journal of General Internal Medicine, 13,* 791–798.

Baker, D. W., Williams, M. V., Parker, R. M., Gazmararian, J. A., & Nurss, J. (1999). Development of a brief test to measure functional health literacy. *Patient Education and Counseling, 38*(1), 33–42.

Barello, S., Graffigna, G., & Vegni, E. (2012). Patient engagement as an emerging challenge for healthcare services: mapping the literature. *Nursing Research and Practice.* doi:10.1155/2012/905934.

Barry, M. M., D'Eath, M., & Sixsmith, J. (2013). Interventions for improving population health literacy: Insights from a rapid review of the evidence. *Journal of Health Communication, 18*(12), 1507–1522.

Bennett, I. M., Chen, J., Soroui, J. S., & White, S. (2009). The contribution of health literacy to disparities in self-rated health status and preventive health behaviors in older adults. *Annals of Family Medicine, 7*(3), 204–211.

Berkman, N. D., Davis, T. C., & McCormack, L. (2010). Health literacy: What is it? *Journal of Health Communication: International Perspectives, 15*(2), 9–19. doi:10.1080/10810730.2010.499985.

Berkman, N. D., Sheridan, S. L., Donahue, K. E., Halpern, D. J., Viera, A., Crotty, K., et al. (2011). *Health literacy interventions and outcomes: An updated systematic review.* Rockville, MD: Agency for Healthcare Research and Quality.

Brach, C., Dreyer, B. P., & Schillinger, D. (2014). Physicians' roles in creating health literate organizations: A call to action. *Journal of General Internal Medicine, 29*(2), 273–275.

Brach, C., Dreyer, B., Schyve, P., Hernandez, L., Baur, C., Lemerise, A. J., et al. (2012). *Attributes of a health literate organization.* Washington, DC: The National Academies Press.

Briglia, E., Perlman, M., & Weissman, M. A. (2015). Integrating health literacy into organizational structure. *Physician Leadership Journal, 2*(2), 66–69.

Bryant, M. D., Schoenberg, E. D., Johnson, T. V., Goodman, M., Owen-Smith, A., & Master, V. A. (2009). Multimedia version of a standard medical questionnaire improves patient understanding across all literacy levels. *Journal of Urology, 182*(3), 1120–1125.

Camerini, A. L., & Schulz, P. J. (2015). Health literacy and patient empowerment: Separating con-joined twins in the context of chronic low back pain. *PLoS ONE, 10*(2), e0118032.

Campbell, F. A., Goldman, B. D., Boccia, M. L., & Skinner, M. (2004). The effect of format modifications and reading comprehension on recall of informed consent information by low-income parents: a comparison of print, video, and computer-based presentations. *Patient Education and Counseling, 53*(2), 205–216.

Chinn, D. (2011). Critical health literacy: A review and critical analysis. *Social Science and Medicine, 73*(1), 60–67.

Clement, S., Ibrahim, S., Crichton, N., Wolf, M., & Rowlands, G. (2009). Complex interventions to improve the health of people with limited literacy: A systematic review. *Patient Education and Counseling, 75,* 340–351.

Coulter, A. (2012). Patient engagement—What works? *Journal of Ambulatory Care Management, 35*(2), 80–89.

Coulter, A., & Ellins, J. (2006). *Patient-focused interventions. A review of the evidence.* London: Picker Institute Europe.

D'Eath, M., Barry, M. M., & Sixsmith, J. (2012). *Rapid evidence review of interventions for improving health literacy.* Stockholm: European Centre for Disease Prevention and Control.

Davis, T. C., Wolf, M. S., Bass, P. F., Arnold, C. L., Huang, J., Kennen, E. M., et al. (2008). Provider and patient intervention to improve weight loss: a pilot study in a public hospital clinic. *Patient Education and Counseling, 72*(1), 56–62.

DeWalt, D. A. (2007). Low health literacy: Epidemiology and interventions. *North Carolina Medical Journal, 68*(5), 327–330.

Dodson, S., Beauchamp, A., Batterham, R., & Osborne, R. (2015). *Key considerations for health literacy interventions.* Melbourne: Deakin University.

Federman, A. D., Wisnivesky, J. P., Wolf, M. S., Leventhal, H., & Halm, E. A. (2010). Inadequate health literacy is associated with suboptimal health beliefs in older asthmatics. *Journal of Asthma, 47*(6), 620–626.

French, M., & Hernandez, L. (2013). *Organizational change to improve health literacy: Workshop summary.* Washington, DC: National Academies Press.

Gazmararian, J. A., Williams, M. V., Peel, J., & Baker, D. W. (2003). Health literacy and knowledge of chronic disease. *Patient Education and Counselling, 51*(3), 267–275.

Gerber, B. S., Brodsky, I. G., Lawless, K. A., Smolin, L. I., Arozullah, A. M., Smith, E. V., et al. (2005). Implementation and evaluation of a low-literacy diabetes education computer multimedia application. *Diabetes Care, 28*(7), 1574–1580.

Halbach, S. M., Ernstmann, N., Kowalski, C., Pfaff, H., Pförtner, T.-K., Wesselmannc, S., et al. (2016). Unmet information needs and limited health literacy in newly diagnosed breast cancer patients over the course of cancer treatment. *Patient Education and Counseling, 99*(9), 1511–1518.

Hasnain-Wynia, R., & Wolf, M. S. (2010). Promoting health care equity: Is health literacy a missing link? *Health Services Research, 45*(4), 897–903.

Heijmans, M., Waverijn, G., Rademakers, J., van der Vaart, R., & Rijkena, M. (2015). Functional, communicative and critical health literacy of chronic disease patients and their importance for self-management. *Patient Education and Counseling, 98*(1), 41–48.

Kim, S. P., Knight, S. J., Tomori, C., Colella, K. M., Schoor, R. A., Shih, L., et al. (2001). Health literacy and shared decision making for prostate cancer patients with low socioeconomic status. *Cancer Investigation, 19,* 684–691.

Koh, H. K., Baur, C., Brach, C., Harris, L. M., & Rowden, J. N. (2013). Toward a systems approach to health literacy research. *Journal of Health Communication, 18*(1), 1–15.

Livaudais-Toman, J., Burke, N. J., Napoles, A., & Kaplan, C. P. (2014). Health literate organizations: Are clinical trial sites equipped to recruit minority and limited health literacy patients? *Journal of Health Disparities Research and Practice, 7*(4), 1–13.

Manafo, E., & Wong, S. (2012). Health literacy programs for older adults: a systematic literature review. *Medicine and Health, 27*(6), 947–960.

Mancuso, C. A., & Rincon, M. (2006). Asthma patients' assessments of health care and medical decision making: The role of health care. *Journal of Asthma, 43,* 41–44.

Marcus, E. N. (2006). The silent epidemic—The health effects of illiteracy. *New England Journal of Medicine, 355,* 339–341.

McAllister, M. (2016). Shared decision making, health literacy, and patient empowerment. In G. Elwyn, A. Edwards, & R. Thompson (Eds.), *Shared decision making in health care: Achieving evidence-based patient choice* (pp. 234–238). Oxford: Oxford University Press.

McCaffery, K. J., Holmes-Rovner, M., Smith, S. K., Rovner, D., Nutbeam, D., Clayman, M. L., et al. (2013). Addressing health literacy in patient decision aids. *BMC Medical Informatics and Decision, 13*(2), 10–23.

Nielsen-Bohlman, L., Panzer, A. M., Hamlin, B., & Kindig, D. A. (2004). *Health literacy: A prescription to end confusion.* Washington, DC: USA: The National Academy Press.

Nutbeam, D. (2008). Defining and measuring health literacy: What can we learn from literacy studies? *International Journal of Public Health, 54*(5), 303–305.

O'Neal, K. S., Crosby, K. M., Miller, M. J., Murray, K. A., & Condren, M. E. (2013). Assessing health literacy practices in a community pharmacy environment: Experiences using the AHRQ pharmacy health literacy assessment tool. *Research in Social Administrative Pharmacy, 9*(5), 564–596.

Paasche-Orlow, M. (2011). Caring for patients with limited health literacy: A 76-year-old man with multiple medical problems. *The Journal of the American Medical Association, 306*(10), 1122–1129.

Paasche-Orlow, M. K., Parker, R. M., Gazmararian, J. A., Nielsen-Bohlman, L. T., & Rudd, R. R. (2005). The prevalence of limited health literacy. *Journal of General Internal Medicine, 20*(2), 175–184.

Paasche-Orlow, M. K., Schillinger, D., Greene, S. M., & Wagner, E. H. (2006). How health care systems can begin to address the challenge of limited literacy. *Journal of General Internal Medicine, 21*(8), 884–887.

Parmer, J., Furtado, D., Rubin, D. L., Freimuth, V., Kaley, T., & Okundaye, M. (2015). Improving interactive health literacy skills of older adults: Lessons learned from formative organizational research with community partners. *Progress in Community Health Partnerships: Research, Education, and Action, 9*(4), 531–536.

Palumbo, R. (2015). Discussing the effects of poor health literacy on patients facing HIV: A narrative literature review. *International Journal of Health Policy and Management, 4*(7), 417–430.

Palumbo, R. (2016). Designing health-literate health care organization: A literature review. *Health Services Management Research, 29*(3), 79–87.

Palumbo, R., & Annarumma, C. (2016). Empowering organizations to empower patients: An organizational health literacy approach. *International Journal of Healthcare Management.* Published on-line ahead of print on November 14, 2016. doi:10.1080/20479700.2016.1253254.

Palumbo, R., Annarumma, C., Musella, M., Adinolfi, P., & Piscopo, G. (2016a). The Italian health literacy project: Insights from the assessment of health literacy skills in Italy. *Health Policy, 120*(9), 1087–1094.

Palumbo, R., Annarumma, C., Adinolfi, P., & Musella, M. (2016b). The missing link to patient engagement in Italy. The role of health literacy in enabling patients. *Journal of Health Organization and Management, 30*(8), 1183–1203.

Parikh, N. S., Parker, R. M., Nurss, J. R., Baker, D. W., & Williams, M. V. (1996). Shame and health literacy: The unspoken connection. *Patient Education and Counseling, 27*, 33–39.

Parker, R., & Ratzan, S. C. (2010). Health literacy: A second decade of distinction for Americans. *Journal of Health Communication, 15*(2), 20–33.

Parker, R., Baker, D., Williams, M., & Nurss, J. (1995). The test of functional health literacy in adults: A new instrument for measuring patients' literacy. *Journal of General Internal Medicine, 10*, 537–541.

Rubin, D. L., Parmer, J., Freimuth, V., Kaley, T., & Okundaye, M. (2011). Associations between older adults' spoken interactive health literacy and selected health care and health communication outcomes. *Journal of Health Communication, 16*(3), 191–204.

Schaefer, C. T. (2008). Integrated review of health literacy interventions. *Orthopaedic Nursing, 27*(5), 302–317.

Schulz, P. J., & Nakamoto, K. (2013). Health literacy and patient empowerment in health communication: The importance of separating conjoined twins. *Patient Education and Counseling, 90*(1), 4–11.

Schumacher, J. R., Hall, A. G., Davis, T. C., Connie, L. A., Bennett, D. R., Wolf, M. S., et al. (2013). Potentially preventable use of emergency services: The role of low Health literacy. *Medical Care, 51*(8), 654–658.

Sheridan, S. L., Halpern, D. J., Viera, A. J., Berkman, N. D., Donahue, K. E., & Crotty, K. (2011). Interventions for individuals with low health literacy: A systematic review. *Journal of Health Communication, 16*(3), 30–54.

Simonds, S. K. (1974). Health education as social policy. *Health Education Monographs, 2*(1s), 1–25.

Smith, S. G., Curtis, L. M., Wardle, J., von Wagner, C., & Wolf, M. S. (2013). Skill set or mind set? Associations between health literacy. *Patient Activation and Health. PLoS ONE, 8*(9), e74373.

Sobel, R. M., Paasche-Orlow, M. K., Waite, K. R., Rittner, S. S., Wilson, E. A., & Wolf, M. S. (2009). Asthma 1-2-3: A low literacy multimedia tool to educate African American adults about asthma. *Journal of Community Health, 34*(4), 321–327.

Sørensen, K., Pelikan, J. M., Röthlin, F., Ganahl, K., Slonska, Z., Doyle, G., et al. (2015). Health literacy in Europe: Comparative results of the European health literacy survey (HLS-EU). *The European Journal of Public Health, 25*(6), 1053–1058.

Sykes, S., Wills, J., Rowlands, G., & Popple, K. (2013) Understanding critical health literacy: A concept analysis. *BMC Public Health, 13*(150). doi:10.1186/1471-2458-13-150.

Thompson, A. G. (2007). The meaning of patient involvement and participation in health care consultations: A taxonomy. *Social Science and Medicine, 64*(6), 1297–1310.

Volk, R. J., Jibaja-Weiss, M. L., Hawley, S. T., Kneuper, S., Spann, S. J., Miles, B. J., et al. (2008). Entertainment education for prostate cancer screening: A randomized trial among primary care patients with low health literacy. *Patient Education and Counseling, 73*(3), 482–489.

Wang, R.-H., Hsu, H.-C., Lee, Y.-J., Shin, S.-J., Lin, K.-D., & An, L.-W. (2016). Patient empowerment interacts with health literacy to associate with subsequent self-management behaviors in patients with type 2 diabetes: A prospective study in Taiwan. *Patient Education and Counseling, 99*(10), 1626–1631.

Weaver, N. L., Wray, R. J., Zellin, S., Gautam, K., & Jupka, K. (2012). Advancing organizational health literacy in health care organizations serving high-needs populations: A case study. *Journal of Health Communication, 17*(3), 55–66.

Williams, M. V., Baker, D. W., Parker, R. M., & Nurss, J. R. (1998). Relationship of functional health literacy to patients' knowledge of their chronic disease. A study of patients with hypertension and diabetes. *Archives of Internal Medicine, 158*(2), 166–172.

Williams, M.V., Davis, T., Parker, R.M., & Weiss, B. D. (2002). The role of health literacy in patient-physician communication. *Family Medicine, 34*(5), 383–389.

Willis, C., Saul, J., Bitz, J., Pompu, K., Best, A., & Jackson, B. (2014). Improving organizational capacity to address health literacy in public health: A rapid realist review. *Public Health, 128*, 515–524.

Zanini, C., Sarzi-Puttini, P., Atzeni, F., Di Franco, M., & Rubinelli, S. (2015). Building bridges between doctors and patients: The design and pilot evaluation of a training session in argumentation for chronic pain experts. *BMC Medical Education, 15*(89).

Afterword

After a couple of decades in which the concept of disruptive innovation became a pillar of management and entrepreneurship studies, in the last 2–3 years some doubts arose with regards to disruptive innovation in business models. Actually, an increasing number of researchers and scholars criticized the short-term perspective of global competition both in real economy and financial market, but nobody can deny that disruptive innovation remains characterized products, processes and relations.

In particular, net society is more and more disruptive with regard to personal relations. Palumbo Rocco's book deals with these last aspects of disruptive innovation applied to healthcare systems. After centuries in which knowledge and technologies evolution strengthen the power of physicians, nurses and other professionals, while the patient had a passive role, the net/digital society and artificial intelligence perspective can reinforce the role of patients.

Before modern medicine affirmation, physicians and professionals were driven by altruistic sentiment to help sick people using knowledge accumulated in the previous centuries and decades of experiences. When the first hospitals were founded in the 15th century, most of physicians and assistant professionals were monks, priests and nuns. At the end of 19th century, began the modern medicine based on positivism. Scientific knowledge gathered through evidences was explicated and formalized, becoming the basis of a new profession that, during the 20th century, showed a trend to specialization (general medicine, cardiology, neurology, gynecology, traumatology, surgery split in different branches).

The unbalance between those who have the knowledge (physicians, nurses and others) and those who suffers (patients) magnified. The patient accepted the diagnosis and cure decided by others. When he or she was not convinced, the only possible solution was asking a second or a third opinion to other healthcare professionals. The medical technologies developed between the end of 19th century and 20th century (i.e. X-Rays, CT Scan, PET, modern digitalized laboratories) produced imaging and information that required doctor's interpretation. As a consequence, the patient remained passive.

In the net/digital society patients can have direct access to information, knowledge accumulated and available in web sites. Some researchers estimate that

79

P. Rocco, *The Bright Side and the Dark Side of Patient Empowerment*, SpringerBriefs in Public Health, DOI 10.1007/978-3-319-58344-0 there are thousands web sites dedicated to health-related information, that can provide diagnosis and cure. The decision support systems and their evolution towards artificial intelligence enable patients to become more and more conscious of his/her health status. This attitude already changed and will change the behavior of millions and hundreds of millions patients worldwide.

The questions that Rocco Palumbo tries to answer to in his book can be summarized as follows. What does it mean "patient empowerment"? Is patient empowerment positive in itself? The book title clarifies Palumbo Rocco's approach, because he analyzed the bright and dark sides of patient empowerment. Moreover, he specified his theoretical framework pointing out that patient empowerment can be disruptive both in term of creating or destroying value. So, Palumbo Rocco cannot be enrolled neither in the group of innovation supporters, who consider mainly the positive aspects of any innovation, nor in the group of those who mainly outline the negative aspects of it, although they recognize that innovation cannot be stopped.

It was much more difficult to answer the first question, because in literature there are many definitions of empowerment and, in particular, patient empowerment (paragraph 1.1). Actually, empowerment is not only related to the autonomous access to information, knowledge, diagnosis and cure proposed by different web site and not even by intelligent systems or artificial intelligence (*e.g.* Watson System), but is related and must be contextualized in different social and institutional environment, in particular health system reforms that define the rules for both patients and professionals.

One way to get the bright side prevailing on the dark one is to invest in patient literacy, in order to enable him/her to distinguish between qualified, professional, accredited websites and non-qualified, commercial, sometimes unverified, and even fake information. Investing in patient literacy helps creating a co-decision system and avoid the temptation to substitute doctors with self-diagnosis and cure. The solution proposed by Palumbo Rocco is to disentangle patient literacy and empowerment, because in his framework empowerment means educating a patient to be conscious and responsible for his/hers health, not staying alone, but interacting with doctors and other professionals. This proposal is insightful for the future, because intelligent systems or artificial intelligence can successfully deal with acute care situations, but less with complex acute, chronic and multi-chronic situations.

The bright side of empowerment is analyzed in a systemic model trough different perspectives: co-production rooted in the service literature (par. 2.1, 2.2), rethinking the service delivery starting form patient needs and expectations (par. 2.3), outcomes evaluation, which is a mix of professional practice, quality and satisfaction (extended concept of outcome, par. 2.4) and sustainability (par. 2.5). The dark side is mainly related to the risk of generating conflicts between the patients and the providers. To prevent this risk, it is necessary to understand in advance the causes of potential conflicts and to remove them.

Palumbo Rocco's book can be considered the end point of two different trends. From one hand, the evolution from diagnosis and cure to promote health, to care for patients. From the other hand, the evolution from technologies as supports or enablers of providers, to technologies as enablers of both patients and providers and supports to better relationships. An evolution according to which care is a result of different steps: to generate quantity and quality of shared information, to control quality of data, to manage big data context, to strengthen communication processes between provider and patient, to share knowledge between provider and patient, and to manage emotion.

Milano, February 16th 2017   Elio Borgonovi

Correction to: The Dark Side of Patient Empowerment

Correction to:
Chapter 3 in: P. Rocco, *The Bright Side and the Dark Side of Patient Empowerment*, SpringerBriefs in Public Health, https://doi.org/10.1007/978-3-319-58344-0_3

The original version of the book was inadvertently published with the same figure in Figure 3.2 and 4.2, which has now been corrected. The book and the chapter have been updated with the changes.

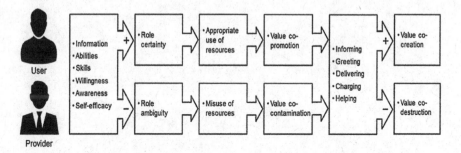

Fig. 3.2 Value co-destruction dynamics in service systems. *Source* Author's elaboration

---

The updated version of this chapter can be found at
https://doi.org/10.1007/978-3-319-58344-0_3

Index

© The Author(s) 2017

P. Rocco, *The Bright Side and the Dark Side of Patient Empowerment*,
SpringerBriefs in Public Health, DOI 10.1007/978-3-319-58344-0

Printed in the United States
by Baker & Taylor Publisher Services